River Tyne Trail:
sources to sea
sea to sources

© Peter Donaghy, 2023
1st edition © Peter Donaghy and John Laidler, 2015

All Rights Reserved. No part of this publication may be reproduced, stored in a retrieval system, or transmitted in any form or by any means – electronic, mechanical, photocopying, recording, or otherwise – without prior written permission from the publisher or a licence permitting restricted copying issued by the Copyright Licensing Agency, 90 Tottenham Court Road, London W1P 0LA. This book may not be lent, resold, hired out or otherwise disposed of by trade in any form of binding or cover other than that in which it is published, without the prior consent of the publisher.

Moral Rights: The authors have asserted their moral right to be identified as the Authors of this Work.

Published by Sigma Leisure – an imprint of Sigma Press, Stobart House, Pontyclerc, Penybanc Road, Ammanford, Carmarthenshire SA18 3HP.

British Library Cataloguing in Publication Data
A CIP record for this book is available from the British Library.

ISBN: 978-1-910758-54-0

Typesetting and Design by: Sigma Press, Ammanford.

Front cover photograph: Waters Meet © Peter Donaghy
Back cover photograph: David Wilson

Photographs: © Peter and Paul Donaghy unless stated otherwise.

Drawn maps: © Sigma Press

Inside cover outline map: © Dave Harrison

Mapping data Licenced from Ordnance Survey © Crown Copyright 2015 FL-GV100032058

Printed by: Akcent Media Limited

Disclaimer: the information in this book is given in good faith and is believed to be correct at the time of publication. No responsibility is accepted by either the author or publisher for errors or omissions, or for any loss or injury however caused. Only you can judge your own fitness, competence and experience. Do not rely solely on sketch maps for navigation: we strongly recommend the use of appropriate Ordnance Survey (or equivalent) maps.

River Tyne Trail:
sources to sea
sea to sources

Peter Donaghy

CONTENTS

Foreword by Brian Burnie	6
Introduction	7
Acknowledgements	7
How to use this guide book	8

The Trail: Sources to Sea

Section 1: River North Tyne

	miles (kms)	
Stage 1: Source of the North Tyne to Kielder Dam	15½ (25.0)	11
Stage 2: Kielder Dam to Bellingham	12¼ (19.7)	21
Stage 3: Bellingham to Barrasford	13¼ (21.3)	31
Stage 4: Barrasford to Warden	7 (11.3)	43
	48 (77.3)	

Section 2: River South Tyne

Stage 5: Source of the South Tyne to Alston	9¾ (15.7)	51
Stage 6: Alston to Haltwhistle	13¾ (22.1)	61
Stage 7: Haltwhistle to Haydon Bridge	12 (19.3)	73
Stage 8: Haydon Bridge to Warden	6½ (10.5)	85
	42 (67.6)	

Section 3: River Tyne

Stage 9: Warden to Corbridge	7½ (12.1)	91
Stage 10: Corbridge to Wylam	13¼ (21.3)	101
Stage 11: Wylam to NewcastleGateshead	10¾ (17.3)	113
Stage 12: NewcastleGateshead to the sea	13½ (21.7)	123
	45 (72.4)	
	135 (217.3)	

The Trail: Sea to Sources

		145
Section 1:		147
River Tyne – Sea to Warden	**45 (72.4)**	
Section 2:		165
River North Tyne – Warden to Source	**48 (77.3)**	
Section 3:		179
River South Tyne – Warden to Source	**42 (67.6)**	
	135 (217.3)	

FOREWORD BY BRIAN BURNIE
founder and Trustee of the charity,
Daft as a Brush Cancer Patient Care

Over ten years ago, I was part of the first pilot walk along the River Tyne to establish a trail from its source to sea. A few years later the first edition of this book was released with all the profits supporting the Daft as a Brush cancer patient transport service. Since then, a lot has changed along the Trail, and also at Daft as a Brush as we grow and develop our service.

When the first edition of this guide was launched, the charity had 18 ambulances and a team of 200 dedicated volunteers. Fast forward to the present day, and we have over 40 ambulances, a team of 400 volunteers (with many of the original volunteers still here), and we transport thousands of patients, free of charge, for their cancer treatment at the Northern Centre for Cancer Care.

By buying this book you are one of the many people who support the charity every day, from the volunteers who give up their time 7 days a week, to the people who donate what they can, because just like you, they believe that free transport for cancer patients is a critical service.

I recently walked over 7000 miles around the coast of Britain and Ireland to promote the fantastic work of Daft as a Brush, with the dream of taking the service nationwide. On this walk I was moved by the passion that people from every corner of the country have about both the great outdoors and supporting cancer patients – two things that this book perfectly brings together.

Whether you decide to complete a section of the Trail, or the full route, remember that as you take your own journey along the River Tyne, you'll be supporting the patients who are transported by us, on their own journeys to recovery.

Thank you from everyone at the Daft as a Brush team, and especially from our patients. Enjoy the Trail.

Brian Burnie

INTRODUCTION TO SECOND EDITION

The Trail has been walked in both directions in preparation for this new edition by the author and several experienced walkers who had previously followed the first edition. This has resulted in a number of alterations to the original text to accommodate official diversions and changes due to landslips and erosions. A number of options have also been included to facilitate time-saving in bad weather or to avoid potential boggy areas. At the same time, a major addition has been the inclusion of a description of the Trail in reverse, that is from the sea to the two sources of the River Tyne. While this 'bare bones' version omits background details, information can be referred to in the relevant Sources to Sea stages.

The Trail has now also benefited considerably from its own distinctive blue waymarks and its inclusion on Digital OS mapping as well as in the hard copy of OS Explorer OL43 (Hadrian's Wall, Haltwhistle & Hexham).

ACKNOWLEDGEMENTS

I remain ever grateful to those who contributed to Brian Burnie's initial creation of the Trail including: Geoff Carrick of High Crossgill Farm and his family, across whose land the South Tyne Trail begins its journey; Robert Charlton, owner of Border Stone Quarry; Gilbert Ward, stone sculptor; and likewise all who helped with the first edition of this guide book.

I would like to acknowledge some of the people who have assisted in the preparation of this new edition. First of all, Brian Burnie for encouraging me to persist with this venture and accompanying me on the Trail once again. I have very much appreciated the practical help with photos and mapping from Daft as Brush Cancer Patient Care team members, Dave Harrison and David Wilson. Once again I am indebted to Northumberland Countryside Officer, Tim Fish for updating me on the conditions of the terrain and rights of way. John Falcus and Tony Aitchison for their friendship and support in checking the walk in both directions. My son,

Paul who played a major part, taking good care of his ageing father as we researched the whole Trail together! The numerous walkers, whom it has been my pleasure to meet, have also made useful suggestions. Last and certainly not least, I must thank my wife Jeanne who patiently supported and nourished me, together with Jane Evans, Steve Cooper and all at Sigma Leisure for their invaluable help in bring this book to fruition.

HOW TO USE THIS GUIDE BOOK

1. Plan which route you wish to follow, sources to sea or sea to sources and how many stages you intend to cover. Note that alternative entry and exit points are listed for each stage enabling stages to be lengthened or shortened accordingly. Likewise 'Options' enable you to choose, for example, between shorter road or longer cross-country sections.

2. Further amendments may be needed as paths may become blocked and landmarks may disappear. For updates before you set out, please see: **daftasabrush.org.uk/tyne-trail**

3. Transport along the Trail will be an important consideration eg: two-car system?; public transport?; bag-carrying services? You may require overnight accommodation; hotels, on or near the route, some of which may provide transport services. See **daftasabrush.org.uk/tyne-trail** for further information.

4. Remember that the waymarks help to confirm that you are on the Trail. They are not all embracing and some may even have been removed or vandalised.

5. Maps are very important. For a broader view of your location, in case, for example, of emergencies, hard copies of the relevant OS Explorer maps should be carried. Hopefully you may have access to OS digital mapping. However, remember that mobile signals may not always be available.

6. Currently there are several places where there is no right of way alongside the river, consequently it is necessary to walk inland and, at times, along roads. Be especially careful on the road sections and generally follow the convention of walking facing the oncoming traffic.

7. Take care of yourself, only attempt what you are physically capable of achieving and that you are properly clothed, including appropriate footwear, for the conditions you may encounter.

8. Please respect the environment in which you are walking by following the country code.

9. Errors or omissions are the responsibility of the author to whom any corrections should be forwarded through Sigma Leisure.

10. **Finally: Do read this guidebook before you set out and remember to take it with you!**

STAGE 1
Source of the North Tyne to the Kielder Dam
15½ miles (25 km)

The Trail begins at the massive stone column on the hillside at Deadwater very close to the border between England and Scotland. The route soon joins the dismantled line of the former Border Counties Railway. After 3½ miles you reach Kielder Village and its Kielder Castle Visitor Centre. From here your journey takes you 12 miles along the south shore of Kielder Water.

This is the longest stage of the Trail and the only one that doesn't end in a town or village. Nevertheless, there are car parks and two visitor centres on route which could facilitate dividing it into shorter sections. You also need to be aware that mobile phone reception is, at best, intermittent. Another thing, don't be fooled into expecting that the waterside path will be flat - on the contrary, be prepared for lots of ups and downs, some of which are fairly steep.

Entry/exit points	Roadside on C200 (GR604974) at the England-Scotland Border some 250yds beyond Deadwater Farm; Kielder 3½ miles (5.6km); Matthew's Linn 7¾ miles (12.5km); Kielder Waterside 10 miles (16km); Tower Knowe 14¾ miles (23.7km); Kielder Dam (Yarrowmoor car park) 15½ miles (25.0km)
Map	OS Explorer OL42 Kielder Water & Forest
Refreshments	The Angler Arms pub and Kielder Castle Visitor Centre at Kielder Village; visitor centres at Kielder Waterside and Tower Knowe

The walk
To start the Trail, you need to climb the short way up to the stone sculpture by Gilbert Ward (2013) which marks the source of the North Tyne. The only access to the sculpture

is via the designated permissive path and dogs must be kept under strict control. (If for any reason the paths on either side of the road should be closed, walk back along the road, go down the track opposite Deadwater Farm and then turn left onto the former railway line – see below).

If you walk a few paces to the right of the obelisk and look down (but don't descend) the bankside, close to the stone post, you should just be able to see the tiny spring that will grow into a mighty river. Now you can begin your own journey to the sea as you retrace your steps down the path.

Ready to start

Once through the gate you will see how a culvert takes the growing stream beneath the road. Cross the road with care as it is much used by timber haulage vehicles. Go through the gate and, with the rivulet on your left, carry on along the designated permissive path with dogs under strict control. Go through a further gate and cross a narrow strip of land, courtesy of landowner Andrew Douglass, to reach the former railway line of the Border Counties Railway. Turn left to begin to follow the 'Borderline – Kielder Village – Shared Trail' waymark posts.

When you reach a gateway, you will see, on your left, the slowly growing rivulet joined by a drainage channel.

Border Counties Railway

This 42-mile single track line, completed in 1862, ran from near Hexham to Riccarton Junction in the Scottish Borders. The track was carried over the North Tyne by a magnificent viaduct with a battlemented top and mock arrow slits to compliment nearby Kielder Castle at the request of the Duke of Northumberland. The coming of the railway, with 15 stations between Hexham and the Scottish border, must have been a real boon to the inhabitants of the North Tyne valley. However, it finally closed in 1958.

Continue ahead and pass the former Deadwater Station, now a private residence. At a gate you cross the Deadwater Burn, which will add considerably to the gradually developing North Tyne. After a further ¾ mile, just after a track comes in from the left, you cross a bridge where you can admire the North Tyne now as a definite stream. However, it quickly disappears from view. You go through a gate and pass Bellsburn Foot Cottage. A short way further on, a bridge crosses the Bells Burn as it zig-zags to add to the river. As you proceed ahead, the North Tyne comes clearly into sight as it passes under a fine road bridge.

Continue ahead on the track parallel to the road and at a junction of paths, bear left along the broad path to meet the road. On the left is the former Presbyterian chapel of 1874. Turn right and walk up the road with care for a short way before turning left to follow the sign to Kielder Camp Site. You cross another bridge over the growing North Tyne and pass the reception office where there is a 'Welcome to Kielder Forest' map. As you carry on, you get close to the tree-lined river before passing The Anglers Arms pub and arriving at a junction where you turn right.

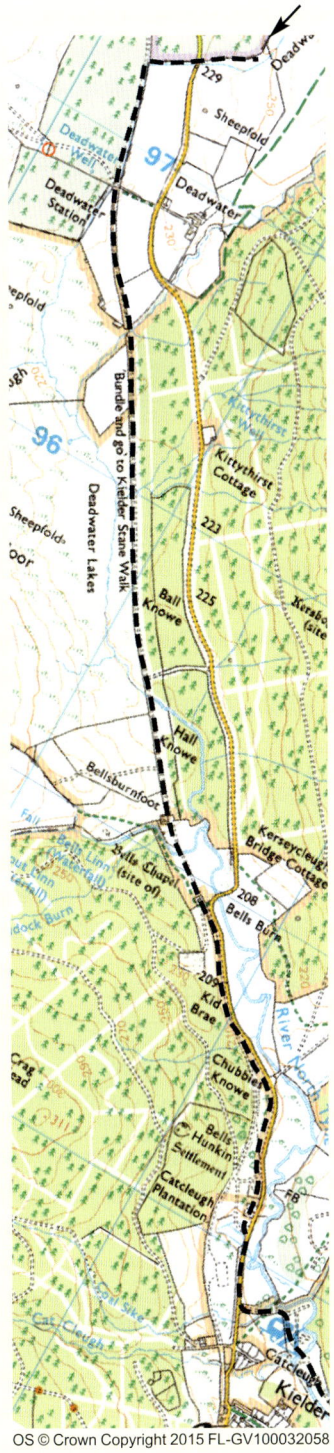

OS © Crown Copyright 2015 FL-GV100032058

Kielder Castle (*Photograph: Graeme Peacock*)

> **Kielder**
> Kielder Castle was built in 1775 as a shooting lodge for the 1st Duke of Northumberland. The first trees of what was to become Kielder Forest were planted in the late 1920s. By the 1950s, the growth in afforestation necessitated the building, by the Forestry Commission, of Kielder Village to provide accommodation for forestry workers. The construction of Kielder Dam, was completed in 1981. Both the forest and the reservoir have experienced changes to their original objectives: supplying water and timber. They have also become integral parts of the promotion of tourism and the Kielder fish hatchery has made a significant contribution in establishing the Tyne as the premier salmon fishing river in England and Wales.

(Nevertheless, you may wish to explore the visitor centre at Kielder Castle where there is a café and an exhibition room. In this case, turn left and make your way a short way uphill.)

Having turned right at the junction after The Anglers Arms, walk across the bridge over the North Tyne and proceed to the main road. Turn left and then right to pick up the Lakeside Way path. The riverside path leads to a road with Butteryhaugh Bridge to your left. Cross straight over the road in the direction 'Kielder Viaduct'. After a short distance, turn right at the fingerpost 'LSW South Shore: Kielder Viaduct'.

The path takes you between two large boulders and then climbs steadily to the top of the rise. At the junction of paths continue straight ahead. (The path to the left leads to the splendid Kielder Viaduct which is worth visiting if time allows.) It served to carry the Border Counties Railway over the North Tyne (1862-1958).

The path curves to the left and joins a surfaced track. Continue down the track a short way and then turn right at a further sign for Lakeside Way South Shore. When you reach a fork, bear right at the boulder and continue on the surfaced track. Keep on the forest path and eventually Kielder Water comes into view.

You will now have walked about 4½ miles from the source of the North Tyne. The river has been subsumed within the vast body of water that you will follow for the next 11 miles until the river is reconstituted as water is released from the dam.

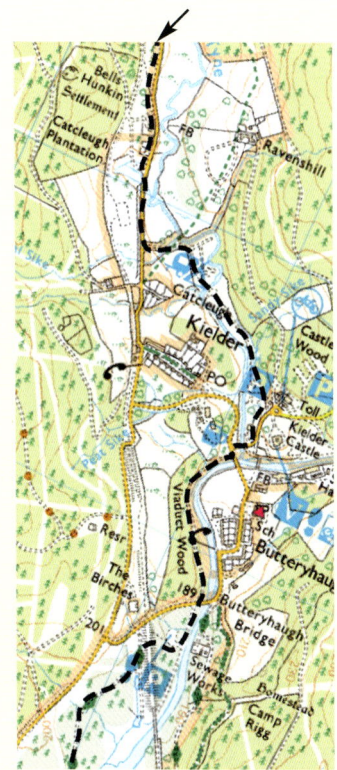

OS © Crown Copyright 2015 FL-GV100032058

Frequent Lakeside Way South Shore signs will clearly mark your route from here onwards. As you continue, your ultimate destination, the Kielder Dam, will be indicated, as will be intermediate points. However, don't be alarmed if the dam appears to be such a long way as you will be taking an alternative route to avoid Bull Crag, which will save you some 3 miles after Kielder Waterside!

Kielder Forest and Water (*Photograph: Graeme Peacock*)

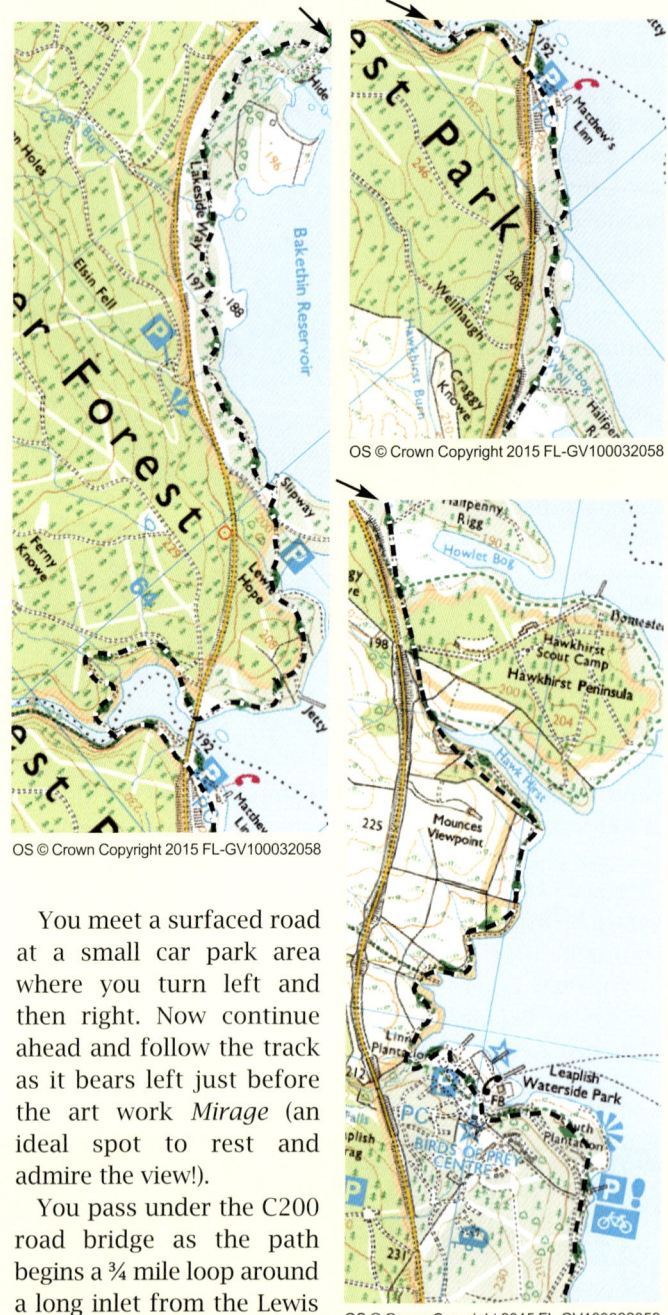

OS © Crown Copyright 2015 FL-GV100032058

OS © Crown Copyright 2015 FL-GV100032058

OS © Crown Copyright 2015 FL-GV100032058

You meet a surfaced road at a small car park area where you turn left and then right. Now continue ahead and follow the track as it bears left just before the art work *Mirage* (an ideal spot to rest and admire the view!).

You pass under the C200 road bridge as the path begins a ¾ mile loop around a long inlet from the Lewis Burn. You cross a neatly curved bridge before you eventually return to the lakeside.

You arrive at a car park at Matthew's Linn with the Calvert

Lewis Burn

Trust activity centre and toilets on your left. After a further ½ mile, you bear right onto a surface track and then turn left onto a shared road which passes the access to Hawkhirst Scout Activity Centre, opened in 1982 when the valley was flooded. The track takes you through a gate after which you turn right and cross the Hawkhirst Burn. The Trail then winds its way to the amenities of the Kielder Waterside visitor centre on your left which you may want to explore.

However, to continue, proceed a short way on the road past the visitor centre then turn left onto Lakeside Way. Follow the tree-lined path back towards the lakeside and at a junction of paths turn right. The path descends to the lakeside and you pass the Kielder Water Ski Club on your left.

Continue ahead until you arrive at a welcome sign indicating that you turn right onto the alternative route (thus avoiding the additional 3 miles around Bull Crag) to Tower Knowe. The path climbs to 'Freya's Cabin' where you can enjoy both the story and the view across to 'Robin's Cabin'. Continue climbing for several hundred yards before dropping down to a junction. Turn right, walk about 100yds and then turn left. Follow the track between the trees until a sign directs you to the right. The path zig-zags down before crossing the Clanecleugh Burn and then climbs equally steeply.

OS © Crown Copyright 2015 FL-GV100032058

Ignore any paths or roads off as the Lakeside Way path leads you on towards the dam. The Trail skirts the woods and you cross an access road that leads to the Kielder Yacht Club. You go over a further tributary (Little Whickhope Burn) before you climb past an access road at the entrance to the Outdoor Education Centre. You begin to wonder if you will ever reach your destination but suddenly you find the visitor centre at Tower Knowe on your left, your last opportunity for an ice cream or a cup of tea! The path continues ahead between the trees and soon you'll be pleased to know that the end is literally in sight as you walk the remaining ¾ mile or so to the Yarrowmoor car park and the Kielder Dam.

Dam in sight

OS © Crown Copyright 2015 FL-GV100032058

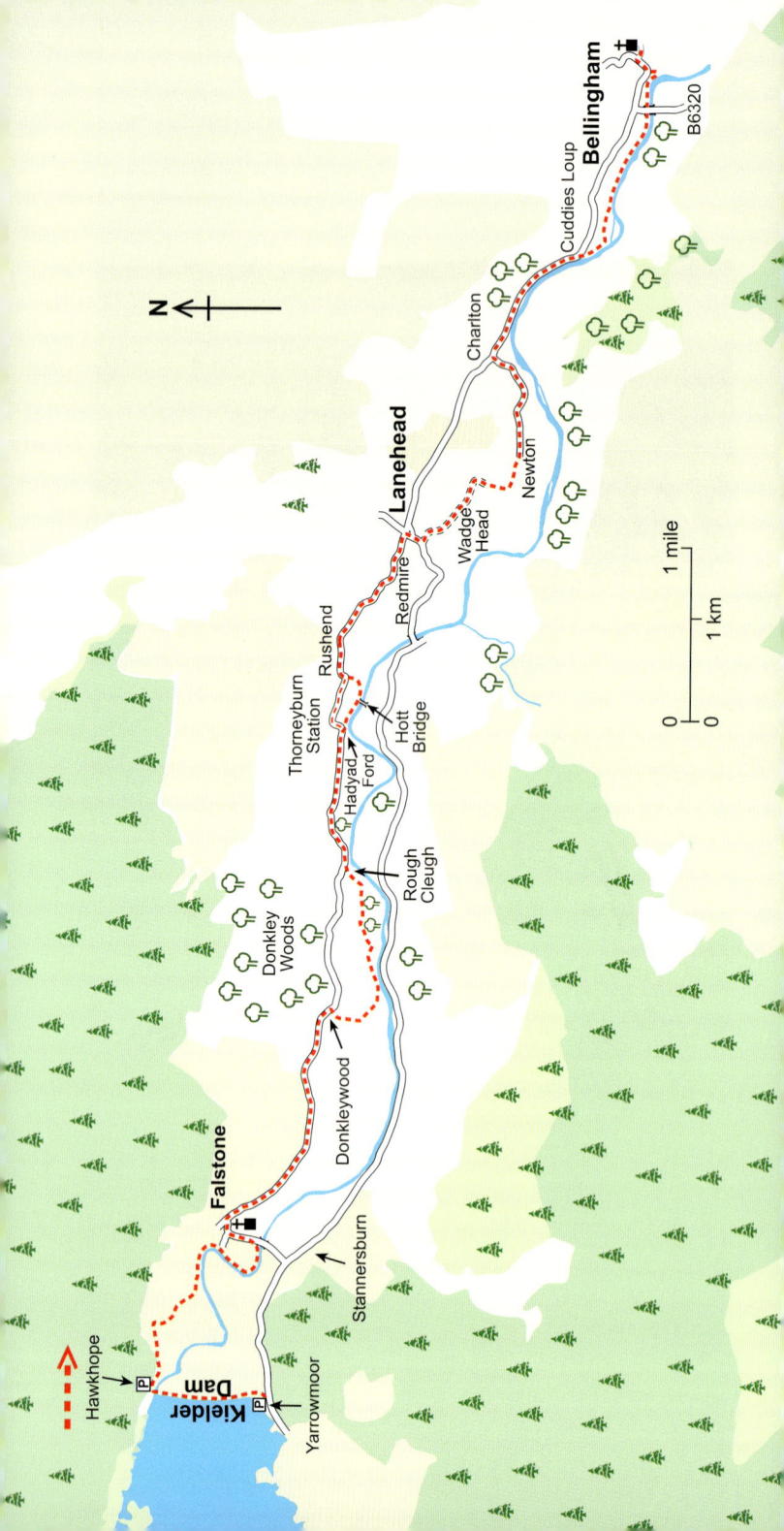

STAGE 2
Kielder Dam to Bellingham
12¼ miles (19.7 km)

The route takes you across a mixture of rugged moorland, meadow lands and tree-lined riverside paths. It involves walking along quiet minor roads and farm tracks and about a mile on a more major road. However, the North Tyne is never far away and there are significant stretches to enjoy close to the river. You can expect to climb quite steeply at times before benefitting from the equally lengthy descents.

Entry/exit points	**Yarrowmoor Car Park (GR707871); Falstone 2.5 miles (4km); Lanehead 8 miles (5km); Bellingham 12¼ miles (19.7km)**
Map	**OS Explorer OL42 Kielder Water & Forest**
Refreshments	**Tearoom and hotel in Falstone; range of hotels, pubs and cafés in Bellingham**

The walk

The walk starts at the Yarrowmoor Car Park from where you proceed across the dam wall. The valve tower on the left controls the flow of water from the dam, while on your right as you progress, you will catch your first glimpse of the born-again River North Tyne.

Turn right to pass the plaque and the stone monument commemorating the official opening of the dam by HM Elizabeth II in 1982. You join a track which you follow downhill until you reach a sign that directs you to turn right for Falstone. You head towards the farm buildings where you bear left to go through a gate. Continue ahead and cross the Hawkhope Burn as it make its circuitous way to join the North Tyne. Proceed along the surfaced road ignoring roads off as the dwellings of Falstone come into view.

The road leads past an attractive children's play area. At the end of the tennis court, leave the road as it swings left

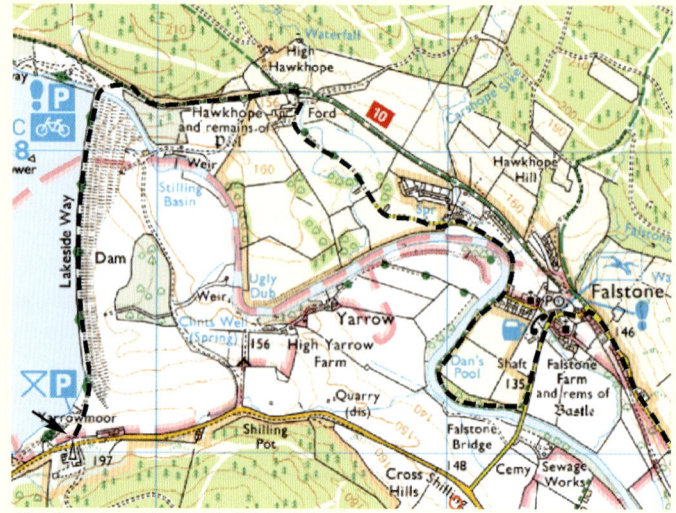

OS © Crown Copyright 2015 FL-GV100032058

Falstone Bridge ahead

and instead turn right to follow the sign 'Riverside Walk and The Stell'. With the river close by, follow the path to arrive at what looks like a sheepfold but is in fact a sculpture (Colin Wilbourn, 2006).

To continue, walk ahead. The path makes its way to the road bridge where you bear left. The path then runs parallel to the road, goes through a gate and winds through some trees until you exit onto the road and turn left. Follow the road as it goes between the Tearoom and The Blackcock Inn.

> **Falstone**
> This is a very small settlement amid scattered farmsteads and coniferous forest plantations. It contains a mixture of dwellings including some 1920s Forestry Commission housing. It offers a tearoom with craft gallery, community shop and a visitor information point in the former village school. The noted Blackcock Inn and Restaurant provides a useful resting place for visitors. Falstone's two other significant buildings are: the URC Church and St Peter's Church (1882) which is believed to be near the site of a medieval chapel.

It then passes St Peter's Church before going under a former railway bridge to reach a junction.

To continue on the Trail, bear right at the junction and keep straight ahead on the road for the next 1¾ miles. It is more like a narrow lane and hopefully you are unlikely to be disturbed by much more than the odd farm vehicle while the grass verge gives you adequate sanctuary. The road climbs gradually and you reach open countryside. The tree-lined valley below is practically the only indication of the river along this section. You should also be able to identify the line of the old railway.

After about a mile, as the road descends, you should see the site of the old station and the bridge over which you will

The Stell

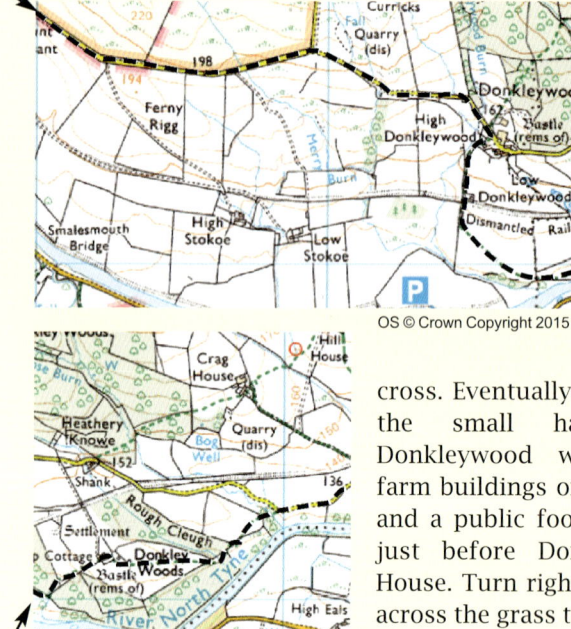

OS © Crown Copyright 2015 FL-GV100032058

cross. Eventually you reach the small hamlet of Donkleywood with some farm buildings on your left and a public footpath sign just before Donkleywood House. Turn right and walk across the grass to go over a stone stile. Walk between the cottages and proceed through the waymarked gate. Follow the farm track and go over the stone bridge with a cottage on the left. The track deteriorates somewhat and can be muddy and slippery.

Just before a stone gateway, a waymark directs you to the left. You need to follow the same line diagonally left, heading in the first instance towards a prominent tree that stands some distance, alone, in front of the woods. The ground may be boggy and the path indistinct, but make your way to pass the oak tree on your right. Continue in the same direction towards the edge of the wood to the wall at the corner of the field where there is a waymarked stile next to a metal gate.

Prominent tree

Cross the stile and turn left. You will now be rewarded with your first good views of what is now a wider River North Tyne. Follow the path, which may be overgrown in parts, between the trees. As you climb away from the river, the path follows the line of a wire fence on your left. You cross a stile which is waymarked. The path keeps about 15yds from the now heightened fence and eventually leads through a wooden gate. After going over another stile, make for a waymarked post at the right-hand end of the stone wall. Continue ahead as indicated and at the end of the property (Camp Cottage) bear right to a stile a few paces to the left of a wide gate. After crossing the stile, bear right in the direction of the waymark and walk across the field. There is no clear path so look out for a stile on the right, a short distance before the field corner, next to a metal gate. Go over the stile and keep near the fence on your left as the path descends. You may have to negotiate a small burn before making sure to follow the fence as it turns sharp left. Climb steeply alongside the fence then walk a few steps ahead to meet a fenced area through which a gate on the left-hand side provides access. Pass through another gate. Now continue with a fence on your right as the river reappears. Go over the stile in the left-hand corner.

Below is a stream, the Rough Cleugh, over which there is a small footbridge. 'Rough' seems a very appropriate word as both banksides can be slippery and considerable care needs to be taken. You need to clamber down to reach the footbridge. Once over the bridge, bear left and then climb to the right to cross a stile in the fence above. Turn right to return onto the narrow road on which you started this stage of your journey.

Follow the road for just over ¾ mile with traces of the old railway on your left. You pass some farm buildings and

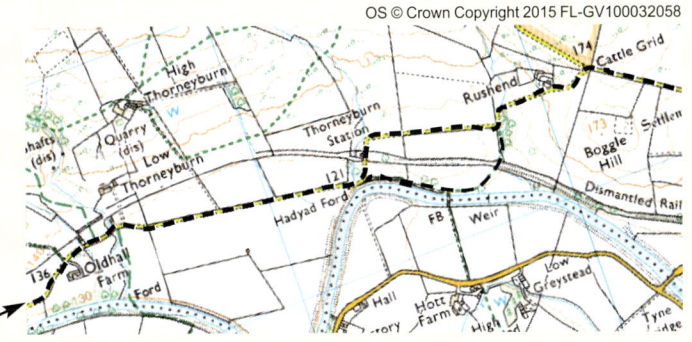

OS © Crown Copyright 2015 FL-GV100032058

Hott Bridge

some fine properties. Eventually the road climbs, the river re-emerges and you reach a corner (Hadyad Ford) where the road bears left. On the right a fingerpost indicates, 'The Hott ½ '. Here you have a choice of routes:

Option A (continue on the narrow quiet road)
Proceed along the road past the former Thorneyburn Station (1861-late 1956) gatekeeper's cottage and crossing gates. After just under ½ mile, at a sharp left-hand bend, on your right, you will see a fingerpost, ' The Hott ½', next to a ladder stile in a wall. Here you arrive at the point where Option B re-joins the road.

OS © Crown Copyright 2015 FL-GV100032058

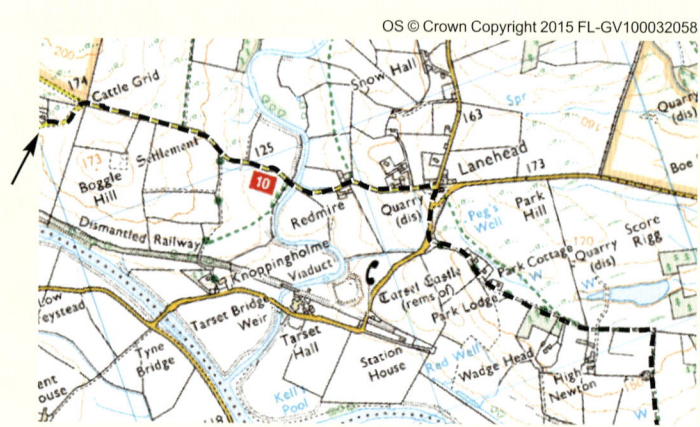

Option B (for the more adventurous with some scrambling towards the end)

Leave the road to follow the sign, 'The Hott ½'. Proceed along the path until you reach the delightful Hott Bridge (1862). Walk past the bridge for about 100yds. Then bear left to follow a faint track up the rise where you will see the old railway embankment ahead. Bear right to make for a tunnel under the old line. Pass through the short low underpass and exit by a gate. You now need to make your way to a ladder stile, next to a fingerpost, in the far right-hand corner of the usually marshy field. Initially you bear left and climb to a small way marked post and then bear right to follow the field boundary to reach the ladder stile. Cross the stile and enjoy the relief of getting back onto the road.

A & B

Followers of either option now continue along the quiet road which soon crosses the stone bridge over the Lairney Burn. The road then climbs steeply past Rushend. At its highest point, the road arrives at a cattle grid and a junction. Having gained height you now descend for about ½ mile and cross the Tarset Burn on its way to join the North Tyne. Continue climbing to pass Redmire as you make your way to the junction at Lanehead. Just before the junction you pass the eco-friendly Tarset Tor Backpackers which opened in 2013. At the junction turn right and walk down the side of the road for about 150yds. This is a busier road and you may need to use the grass verge. On your left, you first pass a road to Newcastle, Hexham and Bellingham before crossing over with care near a corner to go along a minor road.

Proceed along this very quiet road. The road leads past a wood and the entrance to a property (Wadge Head), while

OS © Crown Copyright 2015 FL-GV100032058

OS © Crown Copyright 2015 FL-GV100032058

ahead to the left you can see a pond. You pass a cattle grid. Keep straight ahead. The road reaches a corner where it turns sharply right before coming to an end at the entrance to a dwelling on the right (Low Newton).

Carry on through the waymarked gateway and walk straight down the field. Turn left at the bottom corner of the field to arrive at a bridge. Turn right under the bridge. Then turn immediately left to pass a cluster of farm building and fine properties at Newton. Once beyond the buildings you continue along a tree-lined driveway. The road stretches through pleasant meadow land, bearing right at Charltongate before arriving at a junction with the main road from Bellingham.

Turn right to proceed along this much busier road where you need to take great care and take refuge on what at times is a narrow verge. After about a mile, as the road bends sharply to the left, make sure to leave it to find and cross a waymarked stile on the right, 'Bellingham 1 mile'.

Follow the path, known as Cuddies Loup (Cuddy being a nickname for St Cuthbert). Keep close to the field edge. Resist any temptation to enter the woods and instead follow the embankment with a wire fence and woods on your right.

At the end of the woods, you can get closer to the river and enjoy the views. Follow the field boundary to the right-hand corner where the path becomes delightfully tree-lined. You cross a small footbridge and go through a kissing gate. After a further gate,

Approaching Bellingham

you will see a cricket field, behind which is the Riverdale Hall Hotel, as the buildings of Bellingham come into view. You go through another gate and then walk under Bellingham Road Bridge. You pass a broad green area with picnic tables as you continue ahead with views of the majestic sweep of the river as the path leads into Bellingham.

You arrive at a garage (Riverside Garage). Immediately opposite, on the left, a path leads to St Cuthbert's Well (said to have had miraculous powers), beyond which are steps that lead to the church named after the 7th-century Northumbrian Saint. However, to continue the walk, you need to proceed a few paces beyond the garage, where a fingerpost indicates that you have reached the junction of the north and south riverside walks. You will head south from here on the next stage of the walk to Barrasford. Meanwhile, turn left and walk up to the centre of Bellingham and the Boer War Memorial.

Bellingham
The former market town of Bellingham and 'Capital of the North Tyne', is an important centre for smaller local communities. It is a popular centre for cyclists and walkers who are able to benefit from an array of shops, cafés and accommodation. Further tourist information and cultural insights can be found at the Tourist Information Centre located at The Heritage Centre at Station House, Station Yard where there is a fascinating museum as well as a tearoom.

Happy days in Bellingam (*Photograph Graeme Peacock*)

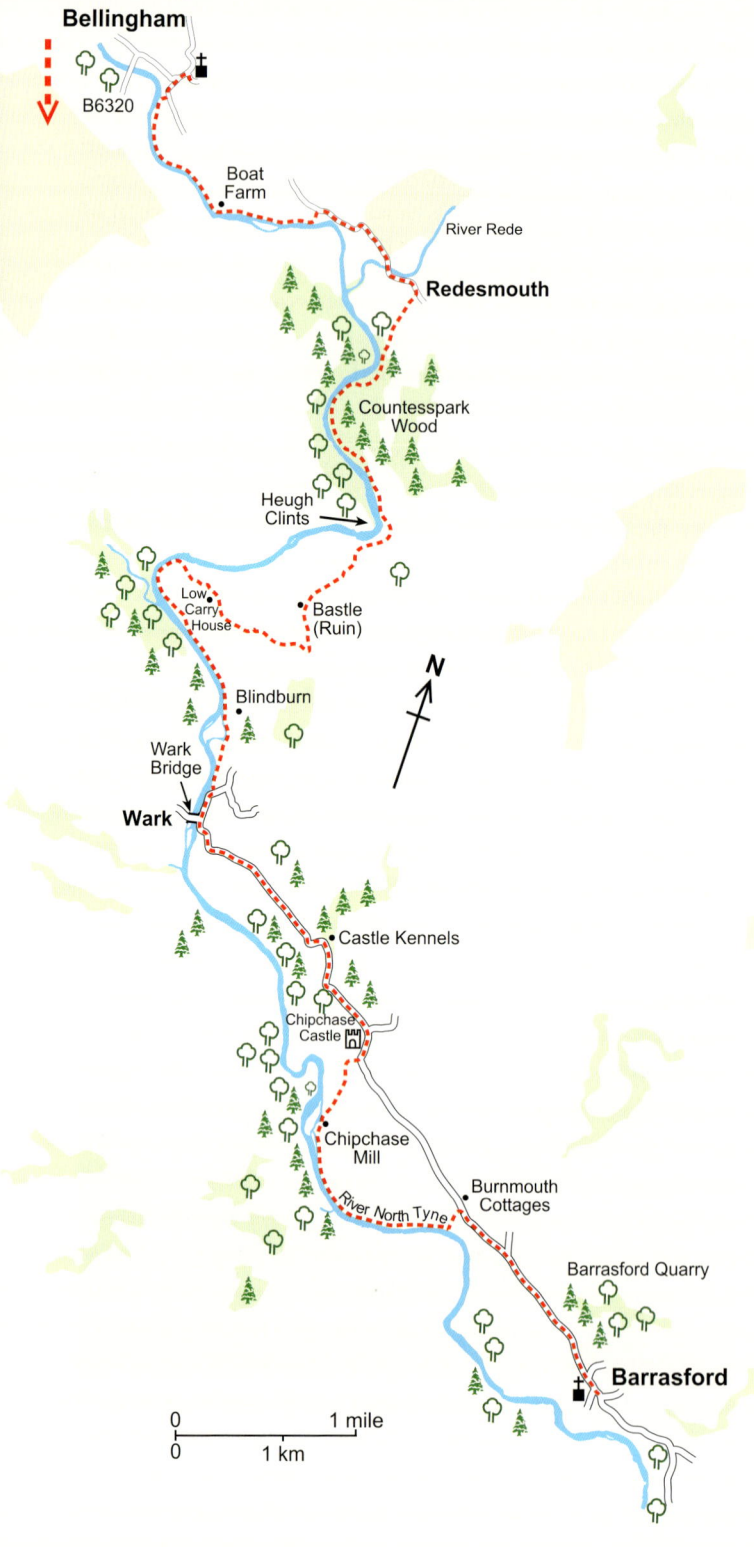

STAGE 3
Bellingham to Barrasford
13¾ miles (22.1 km)

This walk covers a wide variety of undulating terrains: delightful riverside and woodland paths as well as rough moorland. After 2 miles on a quiet minor road leading past Chipchase Castle, a track passes through an important fishing area before returning to the road for a further 1¾ miles into Barrasford.

Entry/exit points	Bellingham GR839834); Wark 8.25 miles (13.3km); Barrasford 13¾ miles (21.3km)
Maps	OS Explorers OL42 Kielder Water & Forest; OL43 Hadrian's Wall
Refreshments	Cafés and pubs in Bellingham; pubs and hotel in Wark; village shop and hotel in Barrasford

The Walk

From Bellingham's Boer War Memorial walk downhill to the Riverside Garage. Here the road forks and you bear left in the direction 'Riverside Walk (South)'. Cross the bridge over the Hareshaw Burn and turn immediately right in the direction of the finger post 'Boat 1'. Follow the path to where the burn enters the North Tyne. The path is officially re-directed past a large property. The tree-lined path passes through a gate and you continue ahead along the riverbank with pasture land on the left. Go through a kissing gate and walk between the trees.

After just less than a mile, the path leaves the riverside through a kissing gate to join an access road. Turn right and walk between two cottages at

Leaving Bellingham

Calm waters

Boat. The road leads to The Boat Farm where you pass some holiday cottages and the river comes back into view. Gates take you across two fields close to the river, until you bear left to join a farm track that climbs up to a gate. Go through the gate onto the road and turn right.

Follow the road for about ¾ miles. Initially there is no verge so extra care is needed . After the road turns beneath a former railway bridge, you have the choice of routes:

Option A (¾ miles continuing ahead on the road)
You cross a bridge over the River Rede, a further important tributary of the North Tyne. The piers of an earlier railway

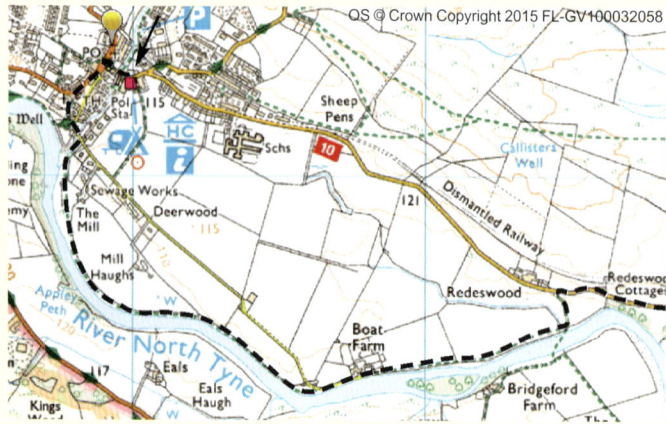

bridge are clearly visible. As
the road climbs more
steeply, be prepared to use
the left hand-side at sharp
corners. At the top of the
rise, a fingerpost on the left
indicates your next
destination, 'Countess Park
Wood ½'. Turn right to leave
the road and join an access
road between the dwellings
of Redesmouth.

Option B
(1¾ miles across country)

Almost immediately after
passing under the former
railway bridge, turn left onto
the byway, 'Sandstone Way
Cycle Route'. Follow the
surfaced track, ignoring
tracks-off and after about a
mile and some steep
ascents/ descents, cross a
stone bridge (Rede Bridge).
Bear left and climb a short
way on the stony track to

OS © Crown Copyright 2015 FL-GV100032058

reach a fingerpost, 'Redesmouth ½', with a cottage on the left
(Crossing Cottage). Turn right and proceed through a number
of gates/stiles along the broad track for about ¾ mile until
you reach the main road where a fingerpost indicates,
'Countess Park Wood ½'. Cross the road with care and
proceed to join the access road between the dwellings of
Redesmouth.

A & B

Followers of either option now procced along the access
road. You soon reach a public footpath sign 'Birtley 3' at a
junction of paths at the corner of a field. The right of way
has been officially redirected from this point. Go through
the kissing gate, turn left and proceed ahead close to the
fence to reach a waymark post. Now bear slightly right to
pick up a faint path towards the far corner of the field.
Descend near the corner of a platform of the old

Redesmouth Station to meet the dismantled railway line. Walk between the former platforms and past two station buildings converted into residential properties.

Make your way ahead for several hundred yards as best as you can. You come to a ladder stile on the right (you'll know you've gone too far if the way is blocked by a gate!). Cross the stile, go down the steps onto a narrow path and bear left at the fork. The path is steep at first and again, at times, muddy. You are now in Countesspark Wood.

The path leads to a broad vehicular track which makes progress easier and you are rewarded with views of the river. You pass a wooden cabin. Eventually, as the track divides into two, bear left on the narrow path which then

Countesspark Wood

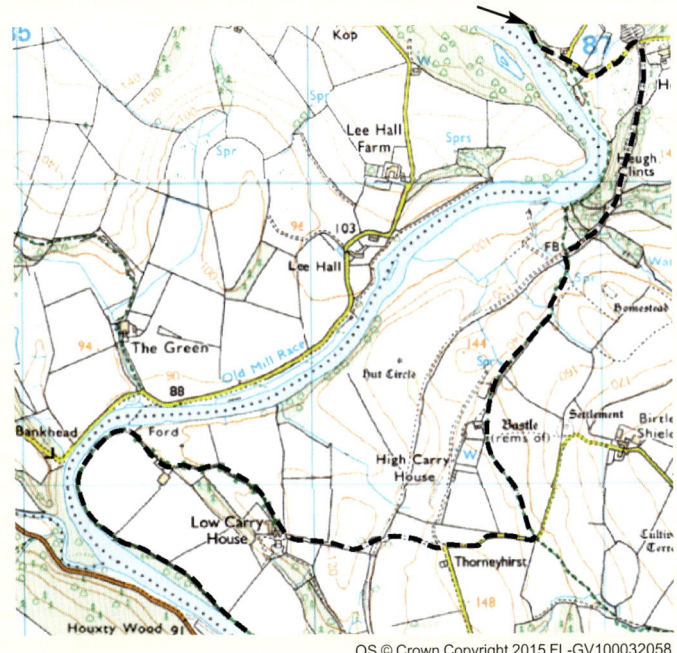

OS © Crown Copyright 2015 FL-GV100032058

leaves the riverside. You cross a short section of duck-boarding and you climb further from the riverbank. The high path undulates but you remain aware of both the sound and sight of the river below.

You pass through a gate and climb gently ahead past a pleasant property to an access road. Turn right and follow the road as it descends to a now-culverted ford.

(In the unlikely event of the ford being impassable, turn left instead of right at the access road. Climb up the road, go under the railway bridge and turn sharply to the right to reach the old railway line where you turn left and proceed as above along the tree-lined track.)

Cross the ford and bear left on the road as it climbs steeply to pass under a gated bridge. A waymark indicates that the route is immediately to the right up the bankside to a gateway. (If the bankside is wet and slippery, you can walk a short distance up the track and then turn sharp right to reach the gateway.) Walk through the gateway to join the old railway track and turn left on the permissive path. Proceed along the tree-lined track until your path is blocked by a metal gate.

Turn left as indicated by the waymark and climb the steps to go through a double wooden gate. Note the direction of

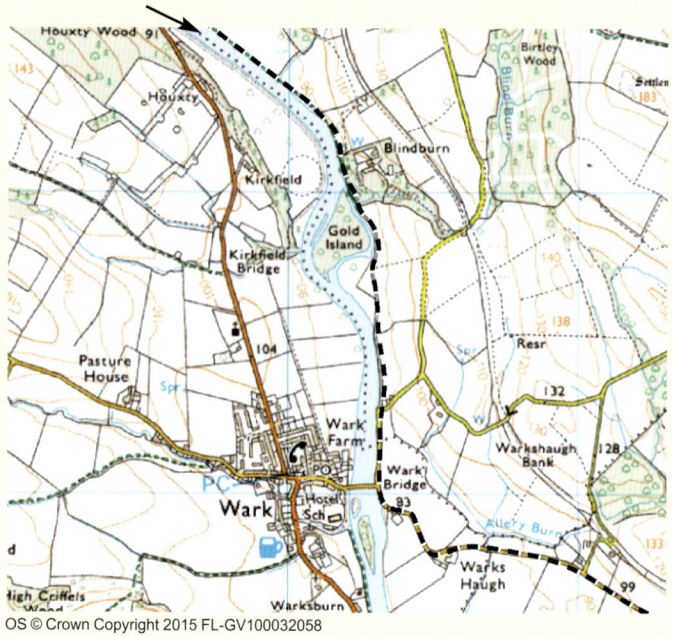

OS © Crown Copyright 2015 FL-GV100032058

the waymark as the next ¾ mile is across rough moorland with no clear path and you need to navigate your way carefully with the aid of limited landmarks. Straight ahead is a clump of trees which you pass on your left. Climb diagonally right (direction 2 o'clock) as you make your way to the brow of the hill (possibly passing a white stone marker). From the top of the climb, continue ahead to the corner of a field where there are two metal gates. Go through the gate to follow the fence on your left with the steep bankside on your right. Continue along the wide expanse of uneven grassland until you reach a ladder stile just before some farm buildings and the remains of a bastle (fortified farmhouse).

Cross the stile and walk a few paces ahead to the corner of the wall near a gate. Bear slightly left towards a distant telegraph pole to the left of a small rocky outcrop. From the pole (which has a waymark) proceed ahead in the same direction to find a fingerpost and a gate a short way to the right of a solitary tree. Go through the gate, bear right to cross a ladder stile and join an access road. You can relax now that you have completed the difficult part!

Walk a couple of hundred yards along the access road to a fingerpost at a junction near a large tree. Carry straight ahead on the byway towards Low Carry House. The road makes its way to the entrance to the farm where you turn right. Walk a few paces, go through the byway-marked gate and proceed ahead along the track. At the entrance to some barns, turn right to proceed along the grassy track, with a hedge on your left, for about 200yds. Bear right towards a fingerpost next to a gate. Go through the gate and turn left in the direction 'Blindburn 1'.

You pass through a further gate and the narrow riverside path soon joins a broad vehicular-style track which leads into a field. Walk along the field edge with trees on your right to arrive at a waymarked bridleway gate. Go through the gate to join the broader track which takes you alongside the river. At the end of the track, you bear right onto a narrow path towards the riverside. Continue along the narrow riverside path for about 150yds taking good care to look out for a waymarked gate on your left into a field.

Go through the gate, turn right and walk ahead close to the fence on your right. Ignore a gate on the right. Continue over the fields through waymarked gates. Eventually you pass a modern property with stables and join a track. The track soon joins a surfaced road and you pass the road

Across to Wark (*Photograph: Graeme Peacock*)

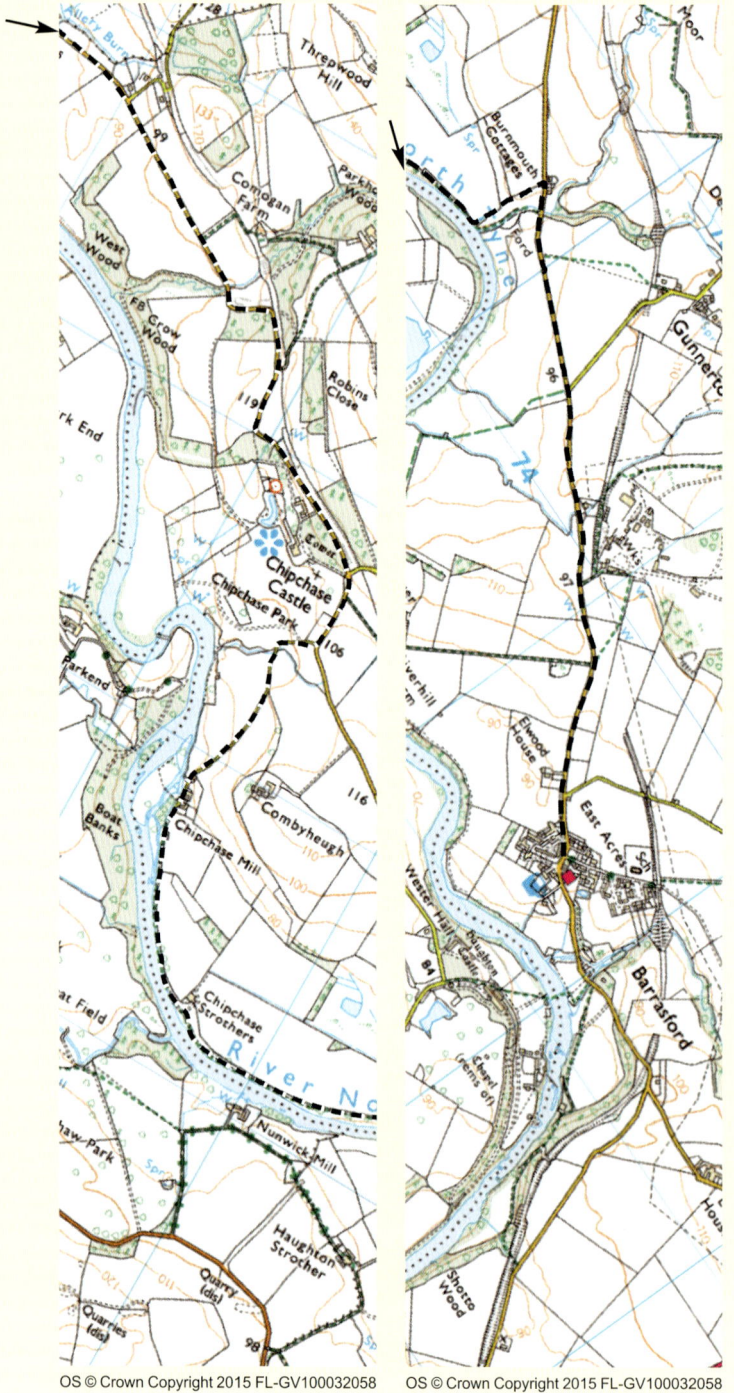

entrance to Blindburn. A road comes in from the left and the village of Wark comes into view across the river. Benches on the riverside provide an opportunity for a well-earned rest!

You arrive at Wark Bridge (1878 – substantially renovated 2013-14) which you can cross if in need of refreshments or accommodation. However, to continue on the Trail, you now need to walk straight ahead on the road for about 2 miles. The road is relatively quiet and there is a reasonable grass verge when required. The road takes you past the sports ground, outlying properties and cultivated fields. Eventually you reach some wooded areas. You pass the entrance to Castle Kennels and then, on your right, the stone wall of the castle grounds. You come to the entrance to Chipchase Castle Gardens and Nursery and then, as the road bears right, you pass the fine gateway to Chipchase Castle (privately owned with facilities for shooting, fishing and other events).

After about 400yds from the castle entrance, make sure to turn right and join the signposted access road to Chipchase Mill. In a short distance, to the right, you can enjoy a splendid view of the castle and the adjacent chapel. Continuing ahead downhill you pass the holiday cottage and farm buildings at Chipchase Mill on your left.

Chipchase Castle

Ignore paths off and proceed ahead until the broad track ends at a turning area. Now bear left along the narrow path which can be faint and very overgrown at times. Eventually the path turns away from the river and reaches some rows of young trees. Originally the right of way continued ahead to cross a stream at a ford which is now impassable. (What follows is currently a permissive path.) Bear left and walk a short distance between the trees to join a wider farm track that swings to the right and then turns left to climb through a gateway onto a road at Dene View (Burnmouth Cottages).

Turn right and walk along the road which may be slightly busier but there is a verge on which to seek refuge when required. Barrasford lies about 1¾ miles ahead. Ignore signs off. When you reach a nice property on the left with white fencing, you will be pleased to find a path alongside the verge that leads all the way into the village of Barrasford. You pass the entrance to Barrasford Quarry, an important part of the local economy. When the path ends at the garage, cross over to use the pavement on the right-hand side of the road. You reach a road junction. The Methodist Chapel (1878) is on the corner and the Village Shop is a few yards further along the side road. Continue a short distance along the main road to the bus shelter on the left, with the Barrasford Arms a little way ahead.

You have now completed this stage of the Trail.

Admiring the view

Noted hostelry

Barrasford

Barrasford is a small, attractive Northumbrian village. Between 1860 and 1956 the village had its own railway station on the Border Counties line. Among other things, the railway was extremely useful to Barrasford Quarry, which remains an important part of the local economy. The Barrrasford Arms is a well-known local hostelry and the Barrasford Village Shop satisfies a range of needs. Currently there is only a very limited bus service to Hexham (Go North East).

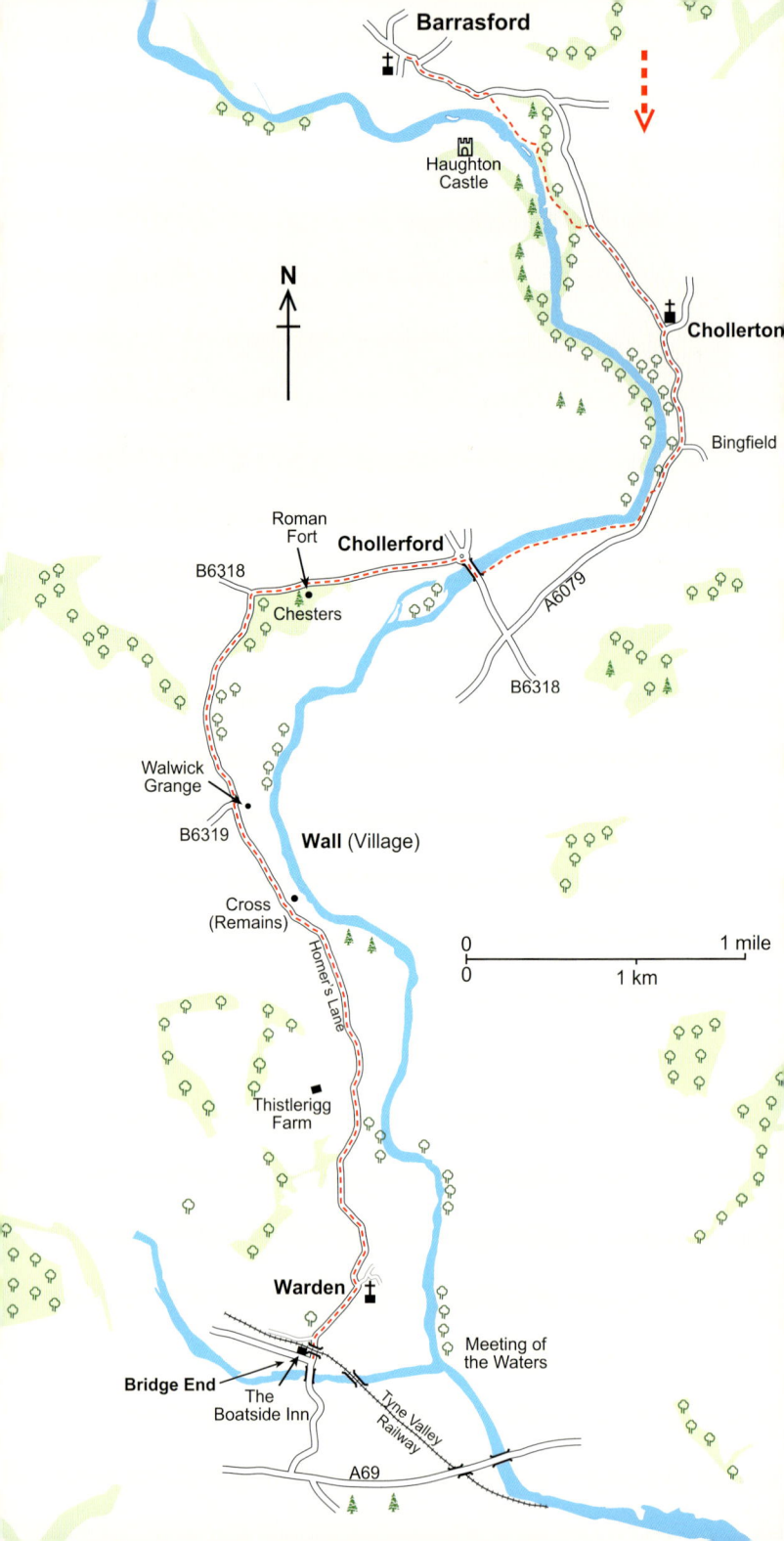

STAGE 4
Barrasford to Warden
7 miles (11.2 km)

This stage continues down the North Tyne Valley with about two-thirds on relatively quiet roads. A road leads to the hamlet of Chollerton where you join a busier road before being rewarded with a delightful riverside section that leads to the elegant bridge at Chollerford. This is now Hadrian's Wall territory and you pass the Roman Fort at Chesters.

The last section leads along a country lane for 2½ miles. It climbs steadily before descending to the parish area of Warden with its fine church and The Boatside Inn at Bridge End. Here you have the opportunity to visit the confluence of the North and South Tyne. With this stage being relatively short you may wish to combine it with a further stage. Conveniently, Hexham with train, bus and taxi links is only 2½ miles further ahead.

Entry/exit points	**Barrasford (GR916734); Chollerford 3 miles (4.8km); Bridge End, Warden 7 miles (11.2km)**
Map	**OS Explorer OL43 Hadrian's Wall**
Refreshments	**Village shop and hotel in Barrasford; tea room and hotel at Chollerford; inn at Warden**

The walk
From the bus shelter at Barrasford, continue along the minor road past the Barrasford Arms. To your right you may catch a glimpse of Haughton Castle (dating from the 14th century, privately owned with holiday accommodation). The road is usually quiet, however, you can make use of the verge on the left-hand side as far as Hatchery House and then cross to the verge on the right-hand side. After a few hundred yards you reach a bridge over the Swin Burn. Ignore the temptation to follow the fingerpost in the direction 'To Riverbank only' (this, in fact,

leads to the landing stage of the former rope and pulley ferry to Haughton Castle) and instead, turn right a few paces after the bridge, in the direction 'Chollerton 1¼'.

Go over the stile and bear immediately left on the path which climbs gradually until you are rewarded with views of the North Tyne as it is joined by the burn. The path makes its way to a broad access track. Bear right along the track towards a metal gate behind which stands a rather substantial and forbidding-looking building. This is in fact a Northumbrian Water pumping station that transfers water from the river to West Hallington reservoir. On your left you will find a little gate that leads on to a narrow path with a beech hedge on your right. You are soon at a stile.

Cross the stile and turn immediately left to follow the path as it climbs very steeply

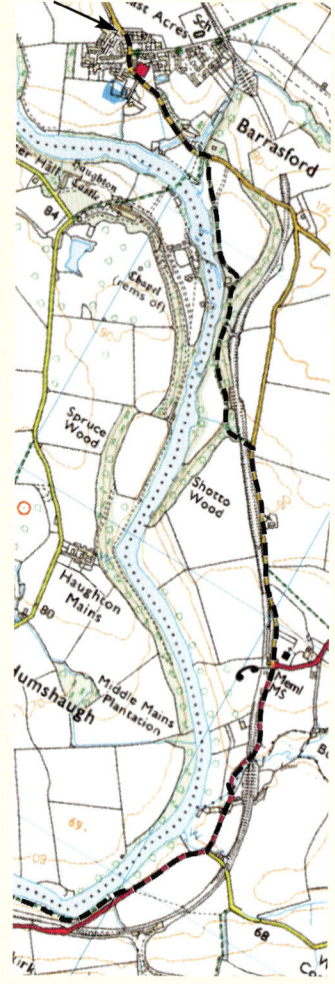

OS © Crown Copyright 2015 FL-GV100032058

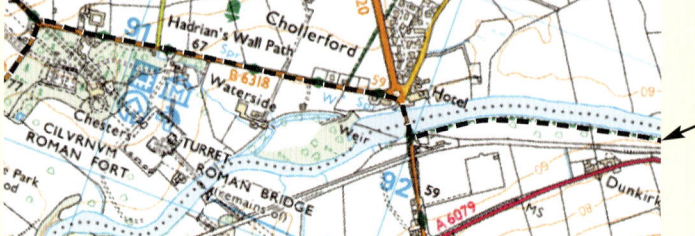

OS © Crown Copyright 2015 FL-GV100032058

River speeds ahead

through the trees. You may need to be careful with your footing in wet weather. At the top of the rise turn right. Carry on between the trees along the top of the bankside. You cross a waymarked stile. The path descends to a small waymark post on your right. From here you may get your last glimpse of the river for a while. Bear left to follow the path in the direction of the tree-line. Continue for about 200yds, until you spot (at times with difficulty) a waymarked kissing gate under the tree-line.

Once though the gate, follow the woodland path, with a tiny stream on your right, as it rises again very steeply and is potentially slippery. At the top, you pass through an old gateway and then drop down into a narrow ditch. Hard though it is to imagine, this was once part of the Border Counties Railway! Bear right and then follow the clear (permissive) path which rises to exit at a clearing back onto the minor road on which you started. Turn right. You now need to follow the road for about ½ mile to a junction with a more major road. Here you find the Church of St Giles at Chollerton on one side, and an imposing war memorial on the other side.

Proceed ahead towards Chollerford on a more main road, the A6079. You need to stay on this busier section for about two-thirds of a mile. Again due caution needs to be exercised. For most of the way there is a narrow verge as an escape route and it may be advisable to use the left-hand side verge as the road descends to a sharp bend and goes under the substantial old railway bridge (1858).

Chollerton
There has been a church on this site possibly since the 12th century and there is a gravestone of that era within the porch wall as well as some stone work believed to have come from the Roman Camp at Chesters. A Roman altar just inside the door serves as a font. The quaint building beside the gate was once the stable and hearse quarters for the church. Inspection of the war memorial indicates the high level of local involvement in two World Wars with an interesting range of regiments.

St Giles, Chollerton

After the bridge, a stream accompanies you on the left and you cross this before encountering the minor road to Bingfield coming in from your left. A straight stretch of road follows. You need to look out for a public footpath sign 'Chollerford 1' at a pull-in spot on the right-hand verge.

Leave the road and go down the stone steps to follow the path close to the high stone wall. At last the river returns into view on your right. The path again may be muddy in places but there is some helpful duck-boarding. You soon find yourself walking along a field edge for quite some distance on a pleasant riverside path. As you near the end of the field, on the other side of the river, you may see the George Hotel, in earlier times probably an 18th-century coaching inn. Lord Baden-Powell, founder of the Scout

Movement, was among the hotel's distinguished guests and it was here that he wrote part of *Scouting for Boys*, published in 1908

Stone steps take you up to Chollerford Bridge. The current bridge dates from 1785 when it replaced its medieval predecessor which was destroyed in the great flood of 1771. A convenient pavement leads you across the bridge. Once over the river, you'll need to cross over to the other side of the road at the traffic lights that serve the one-way traffic system. Continue past (or visit) the Riverside Tea Room then cross over to the pavement on the right-hand side of the road. Now walk alongside the B6318. This stretch of the Trail is part of the Hadrian's Wall Path. You pass some modern properties on both the right and the left. On your left you will see the

OS © Crown Copyright 2015 FL-GV100032058

From Chollerford Bridge

Chesters Stables

entrance to the site of the Roman Fort of Chesters (English Heritage with museum, tearoom (summer only) and shop).

As you proceed, on your right, you pass the impressive-looking accommodation at Chesters Stables. Just before the road bears right, cross over with care to go down the B6319 towards your next destination signposted 'Warden 3'. You pass Gardeners Cottage on your right. There is no pavement from here onwards and, although the route ahead is generally very quiet, the usual care needs to be taken. At a junction where the B6319 bears right, you need to turn left, to follow the sign 'Warden 2¼'.

The minor road, known as Homer's Lane, passes traditional farm properties at Walwick Grange. It then undulates and zig-zags towards your current destination. The narrow lane climbs steadily. After a long slow climb you pass the entrance to Thistlerigg and High Warden Farms. Now you can enjoy the descent into Low Warden. As the road levels off, it reaches an access road on the left where, if time permits, it's worth taking a few extra strides to see St Michael and

OS © Crown Copyright 2015 FL-GV100032058

Waters Meet (*Photograph: Graeme Peacock*)

All Angels Church which has stood here in one form or other for over 1300 years.

The road bears right and continues beneath a railway bridge, this time, one which carries traffic on the Newcastle to Carlisle Tyne Valley Line. You arrive at a junction and on the right is the popular Boatside Inn at Bridge End, Warden. Here your route converges with the route from the source of the South Tyne.

Waters Meet Option

However, unless you are in a hurry, you have the opportunity to add an extra mile in order to view the confluence of the North and South Tyne at the beginning of the journey of the River Tyne to the sea.

On the left, looking at the bridge from the front of The Boatside Inn, a fingerpost indicates, 'Waters Meet ½'. follow the path past Bridge End Cottage. Some stone steps take you to the riverside, turn left and follow the path to 'Junction Pool Bench' where you can sit and admire the confluence of the three Tyne Rivers. Now retrace your steps back to The Boatside Inn where you may like to enjoy some refreshments.

Good destination

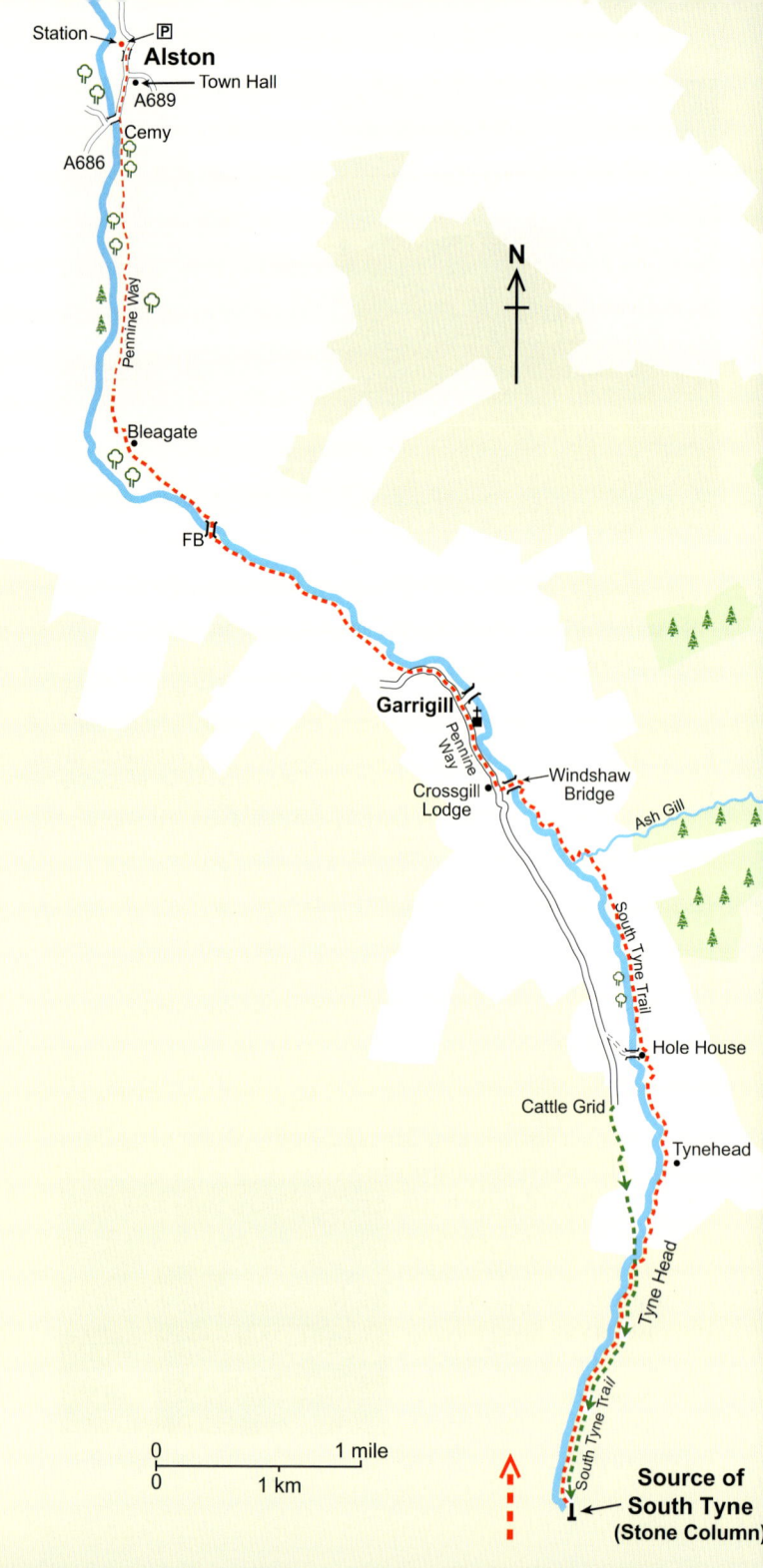

STAGE 5
Source of the South Tyne to Alston
11¾ miles (18.9 km)

Before you reach the source you are faced with a 2 mile walk. Hence the total distance to complete this stage is 11¾ miles (18.9km). Your starting point is at a cattle grid, next to a gateway, shortly after Hill House, at the end of the minor road from Garrigill. From this point there is no public vehicular access. After about ¾ mile you come to a set of fingerposts near a barn (you will return here). A further 1¼ miles brings you to the sculptures which mark the source of the South Tyne.

After leaving the access track, the first ¾ mile is over rough moorland but thereafter you are on green paths. There are only two short climbs but there are a considerable number of stiles to cross some of which are quite high!

Entry/exit points	Gateway/cattle grid at the end of the minor road from Garrigill (GR757384) ; Garrigill 5 miles (8km); Alston 9¾ miles (15.7km)
Map	OS Explorer OL31 North Pennines
Refreshments	Village shop in Garrigill, pubs and cafés in Alston

The walk
The source of the River South Tyne is indicated by a sculpture (Gilbert Ward 2002) and a Daft as a Brush marker stone. You may wish to follow the sculptor's intention and look from the road through the slit to appreciate the beginnings of the river's development.

Now head back down the access track for about 1¼ miles to the barn and fingerpost you passed earlier. Turn right in the direction indicated and climb over rough ground past the large barn on your left. Bear in mind that you are following the river on your left, although initially you are taken slightly away so as to avoid a difficult section. Soon

A wet start

the path descends and, ignoring the gate to the right, walk to the foot of a wall ahead where you cross a waymarked stile.

The dramatic Dorthgill Falls soon appear to your left. Take care as you continue ahead over rough ground to a stile. Gradually you descend towards a farmhouse passing the remains of some ruined buildings before reaching a waymarked gate below the house (Tynehead). Go through the gate, turn right and cross the tiny bridge over the Clargill Burn. At the fingerpost, follow the direction indicated for the 'South Tyne Trail and Garrigill' and go over the gated stile.

Carry on until you meet a wall and a waymark directs you to bear right, away from the river. After some 60yds go over the waymarked stile next to a gate and walk ahead to pass the farm buildings of Hole House on your left. Go through a gate, cross the farm road and go over a narrow awkward stile. Now continue ahead with the river close-by and go over a further stile. Continue ahead and be prepared for another awkward stile with quite a drop on the other side and a stream to negotiate. You pass through a young plantation and the path becomes a little more defined taking you past a series of gates.

Eventually the path climbs away from the river towards a farmhouse but, a short way up the incline towards a property, you need to leave this path and bear left to cross a waymarked stile. Continue ahead until you reach a footbridge over the Ash Gill. A fingerpost invites a short diversion to Ashgill Force, where it is worth the five minute stroll to a bridge from which you can view the upper fall.

However, to continue from the bridge, you need to turn left and follow the tributary a short way to its confluence with the South Tyne. Go over the stile and now follow the tree-lined riverside path. As you proceed ahead, ignore a bridge leading into farmland and continue alongside the

Ashgill Force (*Photograph: Graeme Peacock*)

54

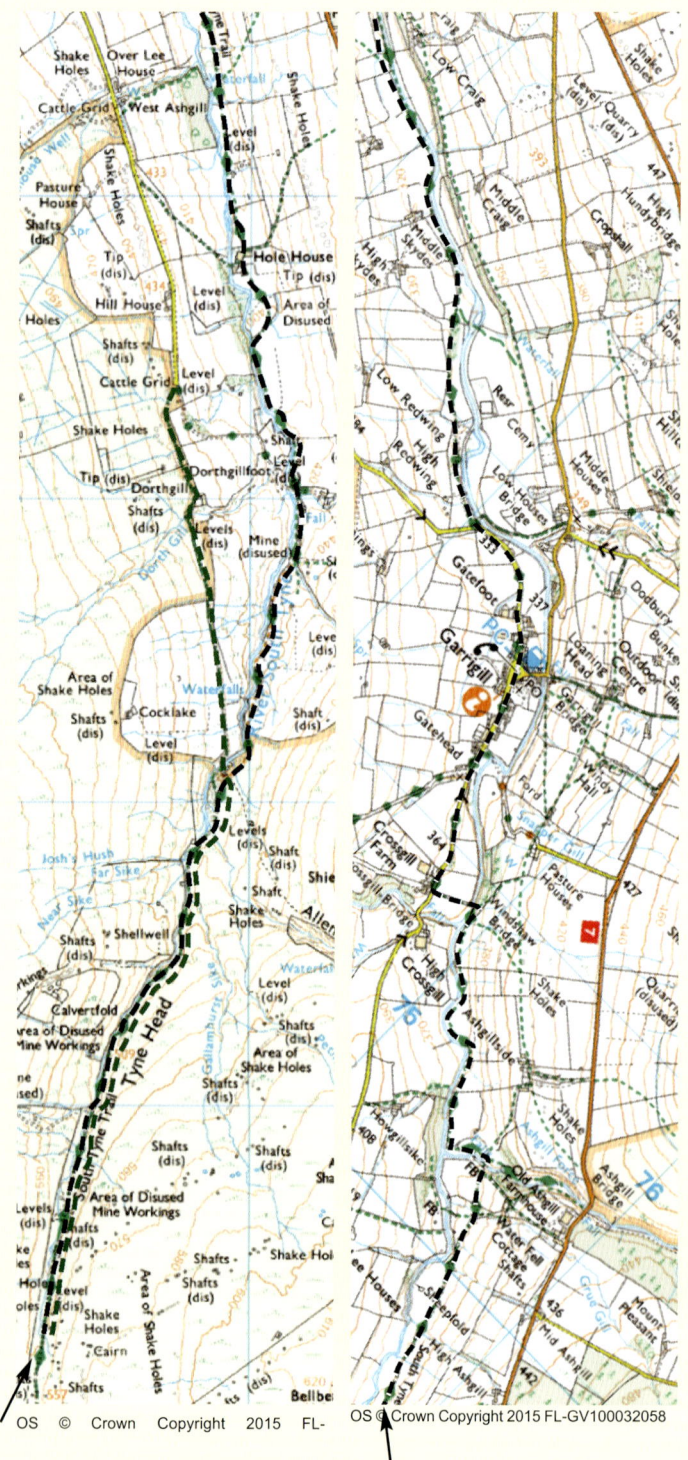

river for about ½ mile until you come to a stone bridge which you do cross. This is Windshaw Bridge which leads via a short path to a minor road at Crossgill Lodge. Turn right and walk along the road for about ½ mile. The road descends quite steeply past the sign for Garrigill. The Pennine Way, which you will follow all the way to Alston, joins the road from the left. Continue ahead for about ½ mile to the village green.

Village ahead

Garrigill
Formerly it was an important centre of the local lead mining industry with a population of up to 1000. Its population now is around 200. The village green, the Village Hall (with its bunkhouse and camp site), the George and Dragon pub, the Post Office (which acts as a traditional village store) and St John's Church all contribute to the village atmosphere and a useful centre for walkers and cyclists.

To continue on the 4¾ miles to Alston, carry on along the road with the village green on your right. The road bears left and ascends. Ignore paths off until you reach a fingerpost indicating 'Pennine Way; South Tyne Trail; Alston 3¾'. Go onto the path and proceed ahead. Soon, on your right, you pass an eclectic collection of equipment and some small spoil heaps.

You cross a gated stile and then follow the path as it climbs quite steeply. You are now on a much more trodden path which will eventually lead you all the way to Alston, thanks largely to the Pennine Way. You soon descend to follow a peaceful riverside path alongside the, now wide, South Tyne. You cross a series of stiles as you keep close to the river and ignore any paths off to the left.

In just over 1½ miles you reach a footbridge. Cross the narrow bridge and turn left. Continue ahead alongside the river for about ¼ mile until you

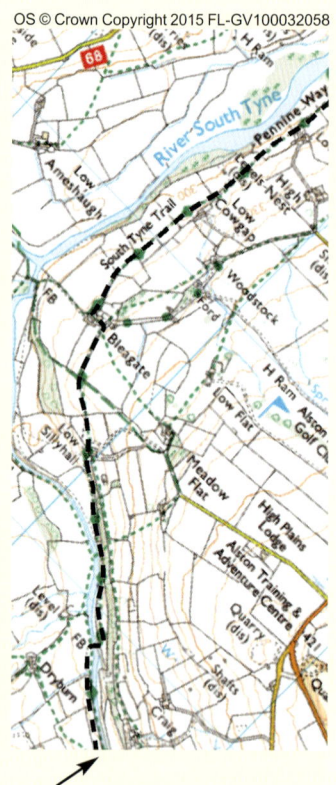

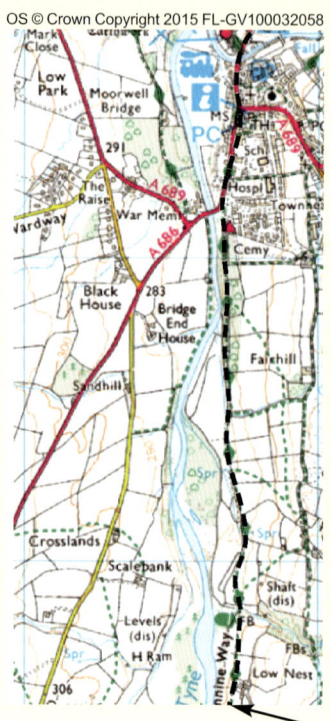

arrive at a wide gap in a broken wall. Although the track continues ahead, after passing the broken wall, you need to turn immediately right in the direction of a Pennine Way fingerpost, half-hidden behind a solitary tree. Now proceed ahead, close to the wall on your right as you make your way to the far right-hand corner of the field. The path leads to a further Pennine Way fingerpost some 50yds from the end of the field. Here you climb steeply to go over a stile in the top right-hand corner. Continue to climb to another fingerpost beside which there is a convenient stone bench. The white-sided farmhouse beyond the bench provides a useful landmark.

Walk to the wall ahead, bear left for a few more yards before turning right through the gap in the wall. Now proceed diagonally left uphill to go over a gated stile in the wall. Continue climbing before the path descends with a wall on your right towards some farm buildings at Bleagate. Exit onto the road, turn left past the house and bear right towards the gate. Cross the stile next to the gate and turn right. Now proceed ahead along the right-hand boundary to go over a stile and then through gaps in the wall over three fields. After another stile you find a stone wall on your left. After about 50yds bear left at a waymark post to go through a gap in the wall. Continue with the wall and a copse of trees on your right, then, at the waymark, cross to the other side of the wall and proceed ahead once more.

Follow the clear path over stiles and gaps in walls passing the occasional property. Carry on until you cross a footbridge. Continue ahead over further stiles. You pass a memorial stone bench on your left before going through a small wooden gate and onto the pleasant tree-lined path. The river gradually appears below and eventually you pass Alston Cemetery and then Alston Youth Hostel. You exit onto an access road. Turn left and walk a short distance to join a road that leads down to meet the main road (A686).

Fine footbridge

Cross over the road, when convenient, and turn right to continue ahead alongside the A686 (Station Road) through Alston. Should you wish to visit the Town Hall (Tourist Information Centre) and/or the Market Cross, you need to turn right at the major junction (A689). Otherwise continue a short distance until you reach the railway station on your left and the end of this stage.

Alston Station (*Photograph: Graeme Peacock*)

Alston

Alston is situated in the upper South Tyne Valley, within the North Pennines Area of Outstanding Natural Beauty (AONB). It is a pleasant little town noted for its cobbled streets, late 17th and early 18th century buildings, the Market Cross and an early 19th century church. It can no longer claim to be the highest market town in England (it is many years since a market was held here) but its altitude of 1000 feet (304m), together with its remote setting, makes it an appropriate stopping place for visitors.

The fells around the town are rich in mineral deposits and mining was a significant part of the local economy for many years. Now, sheep farming, some high-tech development and tourism are important features. Tourism makes use of aspects of mining history and many farmers have diversified, for example, in the provision of bed and breakfast accommodation. Today's visitors to this attractive small town include walkers on the long-distance Pennine Way and cyclists on the C2C (Sea to Sea Cycle Route). The well-stocked Tourist Information Centre is located in the Town Hall.

STAGE 6
Alston to Haltwhistle
14¾ miles (23.7km)

This stage starts from the railway station and its café in Alston. Initially, you follow the South Tynedale Railway, a preserved 4¾ mile section of the original Haltwhistle to Alston line (1851-1976). For most of the route you are walking near to the South Tyne on riverside, woodland and field paths, with just a mile section on a quiet country lane. Interesting man-made features include numerous railway bridges, several viaducts, two castles and the remains of a former prisoner of war camp. For many people the highlight is the opportunity to walk along the dizzy height of the Lambley Viaduct. The walk is generally on the level with the only notable steep sections at Lambley and the National Trust Bellister Estate.

Entry/exit points	**Alston (GR716462), Slaggyford 4¾ miles (7.4km), Coanwood 9¾ miles (15.7km), Haltwhistle 14¾ miles (23.7km)**
Map	**OS Explorers OL31 North Pennines; OS OL43 Hadrian's Wall**
Refreshments	**Pubs and cafés in Alston and Haltwhistle**

The walk
From Alston Station, cross the railway line and turn right. An information panel gives details of the South Tyne Trail and a fingerpost points the way to Slaggyford and Coanwood. Now proceed ahead along the permissive path. Cross the line as indicated. You go over a bridge which takes you and the railway across the South Tyne. After about 1½ miles you walk across the Gilderdale Viaduct which carries the railway over the burn of that name. It is particularly significant in that mid-way across you leave Cumbria and enter Northumberland.

Along the line (*Photograph: Graeme Peacock*)

OS © Crown Copyright 2015 FL-GV100032058    OS © Crown Copyright 2015 FL-GV100032058

You arrive at the platform of the former Kirkhaugh Station, now a stopping place for the South Tynedale trains. Carry straight on, passing a fingerpost on the right indicating 'Isaac's Tea Trail', which 'follows the footsteps of the legendary tea seller Isaac Holden'. Continue to Lintley Halt, which was the terminus of the line until it was extended to Slaggyford in 2017. After a further 1½ miles you arrive at the level crossing gates at Slaggyford. Ahead you will see the renovated platform, booking office, waiting room and toilets.

However, you need to leave the line here for a short distance, so go through the narrow gate and turn right onto the road. Walk down the road for about 175yds and turn left past the beautiful windows of the Yew Tree Chapel, a former Methodist Church, now holiday accommodation. Continue ahead for some 350yds before bearing left and then right to continue along the site of the former railway. While the terrain is level for the next 4 miles, the track now varies in width and condition and you pass through several gates.

After 1½ miles you arrive at the Burnstones Viaduct which took the railway across the Thinhope Burn and over the main A689 Alston to Brampton road. In a short distance, at a clearing, you pass an encouraging sign 'Lambley Viaduct 2½'.

You cross an access road, pass a property with an extensive garden and are rewarded with your first view of the magnificent Lambley Viaduct (1852). You come to a fingerpost indicating that you are 5 miles from your

Slaggford Station

OS © Crown Copyright 2015 FL-GV100032058

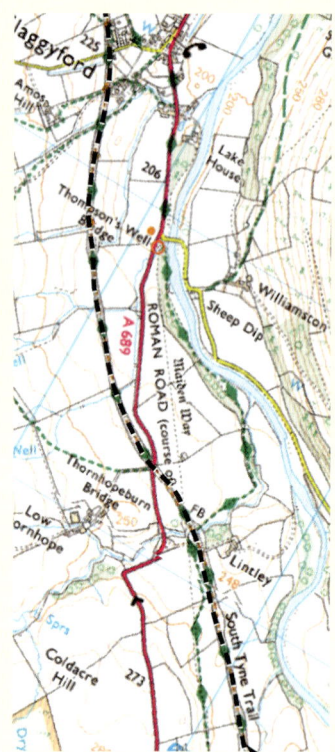

destination (Haltwhistle) and ¼ mile from the Lambley Viaduct itself.

Now you have to leave the former railway track, as the house ahead is privately owned and there is no access to the beginning of the viaduct. Instead, you need to turn right and descend steeply via the steps. Above the garden, on your left, you can see what was Lambley Station. You go under the towering viaduct then climb steeply up the steps to arrive at an important junction of paths marked by a set of fingerposts.

OS © Crown Copyright 2015 FL-GV100032058

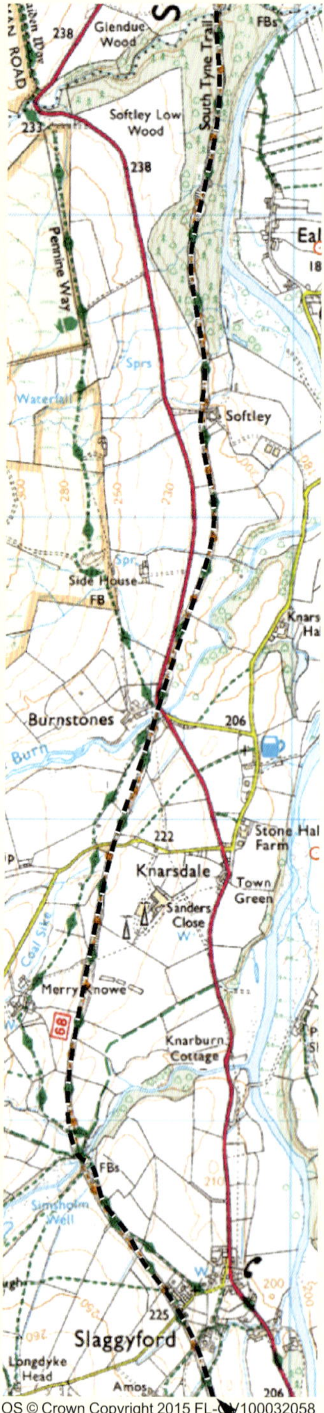

Here you have a choice of routes:

Option A (to enjoy the experience of walking over the viaduct)
Turn left at the fingerpost to follow the direction for 'South Tyne Trail (North) via Lambley Viaduct'. Climb the steep steps to reach the former track where you can amble along the permissive path, pausing to appreciate both the splendid views and the tremendous achievements of the Victorian builders. Once over the viaduct you pass an information panel, 'Welcome to Lambley Viaduct' After about a further 600yds you pass through a gateway into a small parking space. (The former Coanwood Station Car Park lies about ¼ mile further ahead.) After a further 15yds you need to make sure to turn sharp left and go through a metal gate to follow the sign, 'Public right of Way Lambley Footbridge'. Go down the broad track and bear right just before an isolated cottage where the two options converge.

Option B (if you don't have a head for heights or you want to take a short cut)
From the fingerpost, follow the direction 'South Tyne Footbridge, Coanwood ¾'. You descend via steps to a bend in the river. Walk to the footbridge and once across turn left. Walk ahead and go into a field via the metal gate/stile. Continue ahead on the faint path for a couple of hundred yards, then bear right to the waymarked post on the raised

Impressive viaduct

section of the field. Walk up the field to the top left-hand corner where you join a track descending from the right. Bear left to cross a small plank bridge over a stream and bear left past an isolated cottage where the two options converge.

A & B

With the isolated cottage on your left, the followers of either option walk ahead to pick up a faint path. Walk to the right of the copse of trees and then gradually bear left towards the river. Proceed alongside the river. Keep to the right of the trees to pick up a vehicular track and climb up the track to exit at a road. Watch out for fast traffic, then cross the road, turn right and walk a few yards to the fingerpost on the left-hand side of the road. Proceed in the direction indicated for 'Featherstone Footbridge 1¼ miles'.

You now follow the track which soon runs alongside the river. The track becomes more like the vestiges of an access road and you need to be aware of the danger from serious erosion at its edge. Ignore tracks off and keep to the left of the sad-looking remains of a former Second World War Prisoner of War Camp.

After several hundred yards, the path passes a

OS © Crown Copyright 2015 FL-GV100032058

Prisoner of War Camp

Camp 18, as it was known, was one of the largest POW camps in the country. It was constructed in 1944 and initially housed US military personnel before they embarked for the Normandy invasion. For the next few months, it accommodated Italian prisoners of war. However, from 1945 to 1948 it became a prison camp for German officers and high-ranking civilians, who underwent what turned out to be a successful rehabilitation programme.

Former POW Camp

stone pillar on your right, the remains of the original gate to the camp. Make sure to look at the plaque that makes reference to the important role of Captain Herbert Sulzbach. Continue ahead, with, on your right, views of Featherstone Castle, now a residential self-catering conference and activity centre. You reach a gateway which leads to a road. Do not attempt to go through the gate, instead, turn left and walk alongside the fence on your right for a short distance to meet another gate. Almost immediately on your left, you will see the pedestrian bridge, which you are not going to cross!.

Go through the gate to join a road. Turn left to walk along this pleasant and normally quiet country lane for about a mile. You pass the splendid mid-19th century Featherstone Bridge on your left. Proceed ahead and, just after passing

Featherstone Castle

the Camping and Caravanning Club site on the left, you come to the National Trust Bellister Estate information panel. This describes a permissive circular walk through the estate. You can now make use of the easterly section to take you to Haltwhistle (should it be closed, you would need to proceed up the road). Care is needed in several places where the path is narrow and there is evidence of erosion. There are some steep inclines. Go through the gate and follow the narrow path straight ahead. Ignore any paths off. This ancient woodland is a real treat for nature lovers with its abundant wild flowers.

Eventually when you are high above the river the path leads through a gate. Turn left, follow the fence for a short distance but make sure to turn right at the waymark and climb ahead, taking care over an eroded section, to go through a gate. Thereafter continue to enjoy the woodland. When you reach high ground where the path is fenced on both sides, you should be able to obtain a view of the river as it flows to the road bridge over the A69 with Haltwhistle beyond.

Eventually, you come to an inviting bench and a plaque inscribed with a poem *Nature's Magic*. Turn left at the junction of paths, walk downhill with a road nearby to your right and then descend via a series of steep steps to the riverside. Continue ahead on the pleasant path. Beyond the road on your right, you may be able to see the ruins of the

14th-century Bellister Castle, which is attached to a 19th-century mansion house.

At a power line, just before the bridge which carries the A69 Haltwhistle Bypass over the river, turn right to leave the riverside. Follow the stepped path to an access road and a fingerpost 'Bellister Bank ½'. (Note that Stage 7 returns to this point from Haltwhistle. However, if you decide not to stop at Haltwhistle, turn right here and follow Stage 7 from page 75).

To proceed to Haltwhistle, turn left and go under the A69 bridge. Here you have a choice of routes depending on time available and weather.

Option A (riverside path liable to flooding after rain)
After about 40yds beyond the road bridge turn left at a fingerpost, 'Bellister Haugh ½'. Go through the gap in the fence and follow the path down to the riverside. Follow the path downstream, climbing after about 100yds to cross over an access road and then back down to the riverside. Continue on the riverside path for a further 700yds or so before leaving the riverside to climb to the end of a bridge. Turn left, walk across the bridge and go under the Boat Lane railway bridge to arrive at a road junction.

OS © Crown Copyright 2015 FL-GV100032058

Option B (quiet old road, Bellister Road)

After going under A69 road bridge, continue ahead on the old road for about half a mile. Ignore paths off until you pass a property where you turn left and cross a bridge over the South Tyne and go under the Boat Lane railway bridge to arrive at a road junction.

A & B

Followers of either option turn left at the road junction. Proceed a short distance, and at a crossroads, turn left into Haltwhistle station car park and the end of this stage The town centre and amenities lie very close at hand.

A69 before Haltwhistle

Haltwhistle

Haltwhistle is a small and pleasant Northumbrian town. Light industries are located away from the centre, which remains unspoilt. However, it is tourism which now provides the most substantial input into the local economy and walking festivals have proved to be very popular.

Town inhabitants are proud of claims for Haltwhistle to be the centre of Britain and, understandably, it features heavily in promoting the town. It is only fair to point out that other locations have been suggested as the centre but local citizens will, no doubt, continue to defend their claim.

Haltwhistle (*Photograph: Graeme Peacock*)

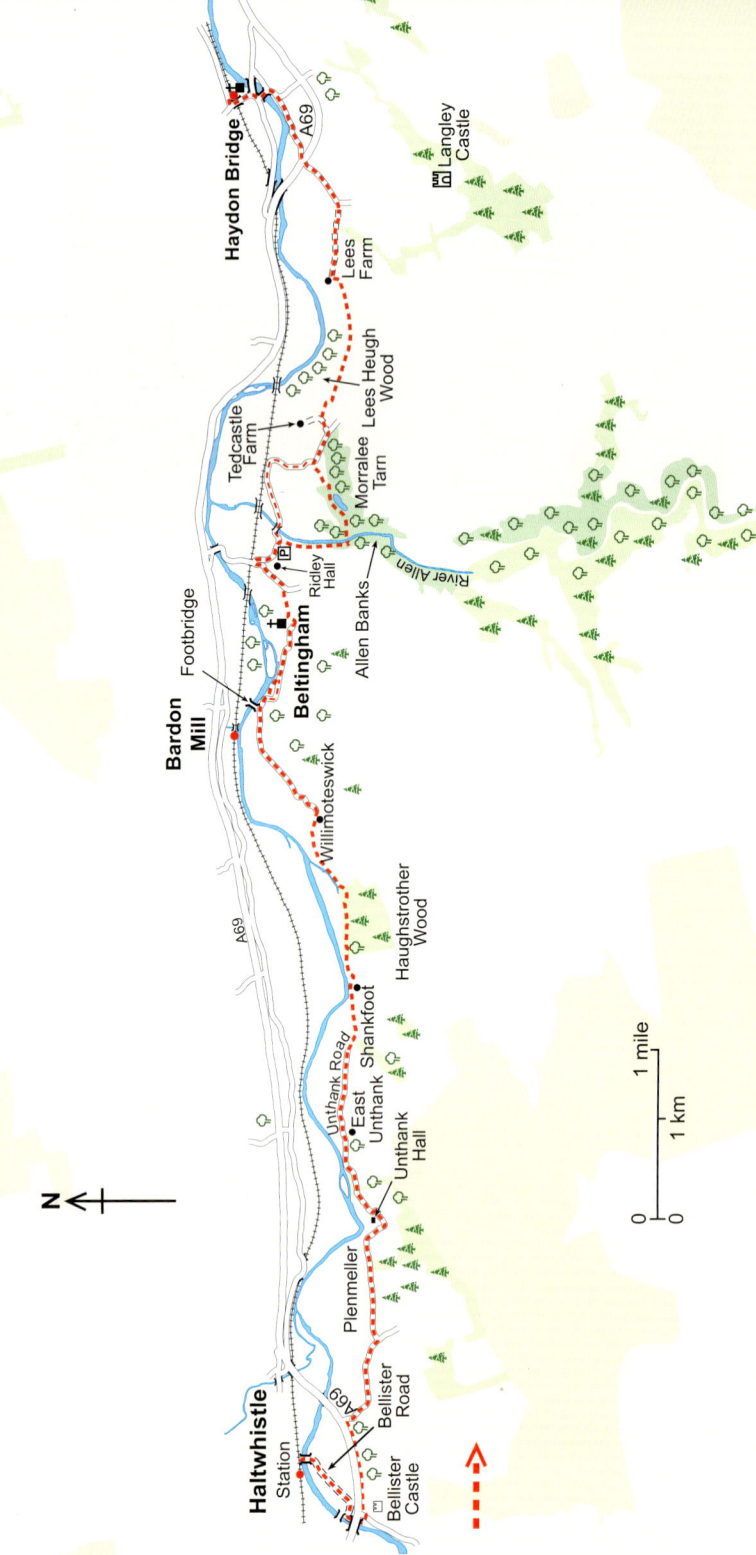

STAGE 7
Haltwhistle to Haydon Bridge
13¼ miles (21.3km)

Although there is only limited direct riverside walking, there are many fine views of the South Tyne. You walk through some attractive wooded areas and open countryside with some steep climbs and a number of quiet road sections. Interesting features on route include an impressive castle gatehouse, a charming old church associated with a 7th-century northern saint, as well as a 20th-century member of the Royal Family.

Entry/exit points	**Haltwhistle (GR704638); Bardon Mill 7 miles (11.2km)); National Trust car park at Allen Banks 8.5 miles (13.7km); Haydon Bridge 13.25 miles (21.3km)**
Map	**OS Explorer OL43 Hadrian's Wall**
Refreshments	**Haltwhistle, Bardon Mill and Haydon Bridge**

The walk
From Haltwhistle railway station, walk to the crossroads, with The Railway Inn just beyond, and turn right. (From Platform 2 you can access the Trail directly by following the sign, 'Way out avoiding footbridge'.) Proceed a short way before turning right to go under the railway line at Boat Lane. A bridge then takes you over the South Tyne. Here you have a choice of routes:

Option A (riverside path liable to flooding after very heavy rain)
Turn immediately right at the end of the bridge and make your way down the stony path to the riverside. Follow the river upstream for about 700yds. Just before a bridge (Bellister Bridge), you need to bear left to climb past a fingerpost, go over an access road and descend back to the riverside path. After a further 100yds or so, just before a further bridge (A69), you need to turn left up a stony path.

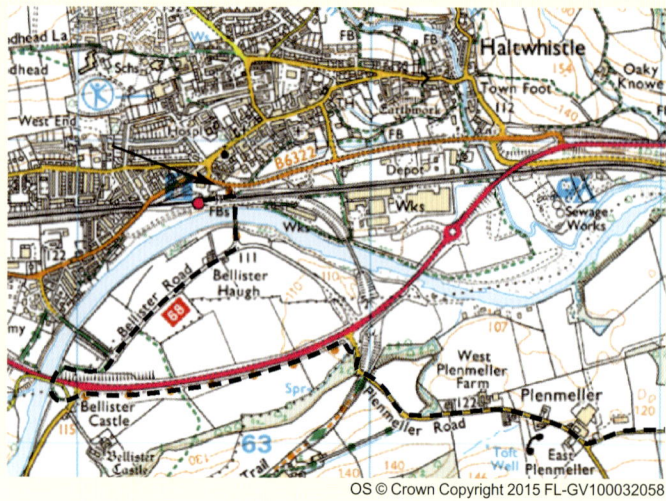

OS © Crown Copyright 2015 FL-GV100032058

Go through a gap in the fence and join an old road (Bellister Road) at the fingerpost, 'Bellister Haugh ½'. Turn right and walk a few yards to the bridge under the A69.

Option B (on very quiet access road)
After crossing the bridge over the South Tyne, continue ahead to a junction. Turn right and proceed along the old road (Bellister Road), for about a half a mile, ignoring paths off, to the bridge under the A69.

Bellister Castle

A & B

Followers of either option walk under the A69, the old road bears left (on your right you will see a fingerpost, 'Bellister Bank ½' (marking the point you arrived at from Alston on Stage 6). However, continue along the road past a gate and then a further gate next to a cattle grid and a Cycleway 68 sign. Cross over the road and go through a gateway. The ruins of Bellister Castle lie ahead. You need to turn immediately left and proceed along the permissive 68 cycleway track parallel to the A69. Exit via a gate onto a road (Plenmeller Road). Turn right and continue along this minor road for about ¾ mile. You pass through pleasant farmland with the scattered, and at times, substantial dwellings of Plenmeller. At a junction, turn left at the fingerpost, 'Unthank – No through road'. You are about to follow this thankless road for the next 2.75 miles!

Initially, the road stretches almost straight ahead for about ¾ mile before bearing right and then left past some delightful cottages, the austere-looking Unthank Hall and the adjacent farm buildings. Ignore the public footpath ahead and instead follow the road as it descends to the left. You pass the remains of a walled garden. Eventually, just before East Unthank Farm, the road bears left over a cattle grid.

`As you continue, you pass some barns and outbuildings at Shankfoot where the road bends sharply to the right. Climb between the farm buildings and turn left to cross a stone bridge and a cattle grid. Now keep straight ahead on the track, ignoring paths off and keeping to the field edge, until a gate leads into Haughstrother Wood.

Proceed ahead along the forest track which may be churned and rutted. At a junction keep straight ahead on

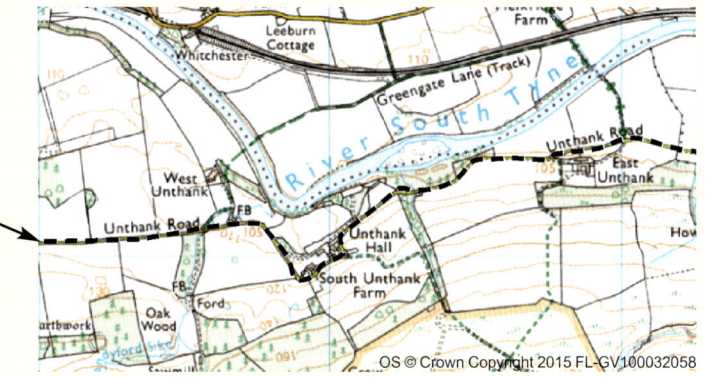

Through the woods

the main track which climbs steadily. Eventually the track descends to exit from the woods at a gate. The river becomes visible ahead. In a short distance, bear right to join a surfaced access track. Follow the track for about 150yds, go over a waymarked stile and pass outbuildings and a cottage to join a further vehicular track. After a level section, the track climbs steadily up to the impressive castle gatehouse and farm of Willimoteswick. (A 16th-century fortified manor house, once the principal residence of the Ridley family. The curious name is thought to be derived from either 'guillemot' or 'William'.)

Turn left at the farm buildings to join a minor road and bear left down the road. You pass the aptly-named Bridge Cottage as you cross the Willimoteswick Burn making its way

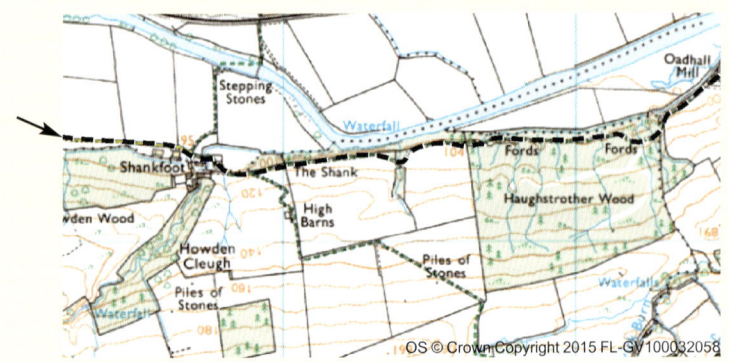

Steady climb

to join the South Tyne. After about ¾ mile you reach a clearing on your left, behind which there is a footbridge over the river. Walk towards the footbridge but do not cross it unless you wish to go an extra ¼ mile to the village of Bardon Mill where you will find Bardon Mill Railway Station, the Village Shop and Tearoom, the Bowes Hotel and several B&Bs.

Here you have a choice of routes:

Option A (riverside and woodland path, courtesy of Northumberland Wildlife Nature Reserves)
Bear left from the bridge and follow the narrow path which leads into the Nature Reserve. The path soon reaches the riverside. Make your way ahead close to the river, taking care of tree roots and overhanging branches. You arrive at

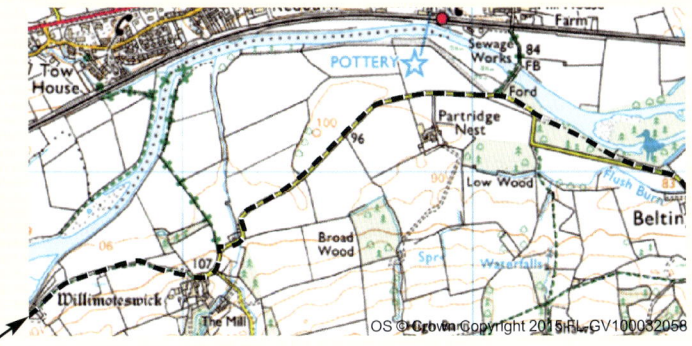

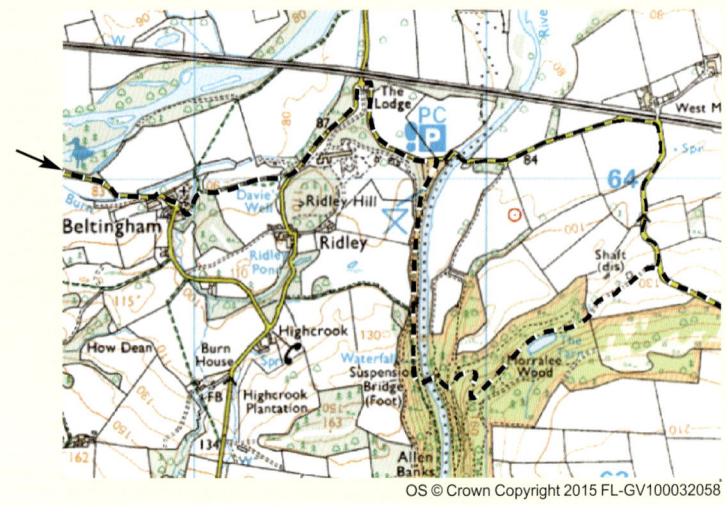

OS © Crown Copyright 2015 FL-GV100032058

a clearing where you need to take a path on your right to pass an information panel, 'Calaminarian Grassland'. Exit through the gate back onto the minor road. Turn left and follow the road as described below.

Option B (continue ahead on the minor road, which may be advisable after heavy rain)
After about ¼ mile you pass the exit gate from the Nature Reserve.

A & B
Both routes continue along the road which after a while rises quite steeply into Beltingham. Take special care at the sharp corner as you reach the top of the rise. The road arrives at a church and a cluster of attractive dwellings. Just

Beltingham
On your left you pass the charming old church dedicated to St Cuthbert, yet another site claimed to be a resting place of the saint's body on its 9th-century journey from Lindisfarne to Durham. A more modern association is with the family of the late Queen Elizabeth the Queen Mother (1900-2002), the Bowes-Lyons. An enclosed corner of the graveyard is reserved for the family. There are some delightful properties including Beltingham House on the right with the Bowes-Lyon family initials engraved in the stone work.

St Cuthbert's Beltingham (*Photograph: Graeme Peacock*)

a few strides beyond the church, take care to spot a post box on the left and a fingerpost, 'Ridley ¼; Ridley Bridge ¾'.

Turn left at the post box and follow the path as it descends to cross a burn before rising steeply between the trees and passing through a kissing gate. Continue along the top of the field keeping close to the fence on your right. You climb to a gate after which you arrive at a road. Turn left and follow the road as it descends to a junction at the entrance to Ridley Hall (once owned by the Bowes-Lyon Family, until 2017 used as a boarding school, now privately owned).

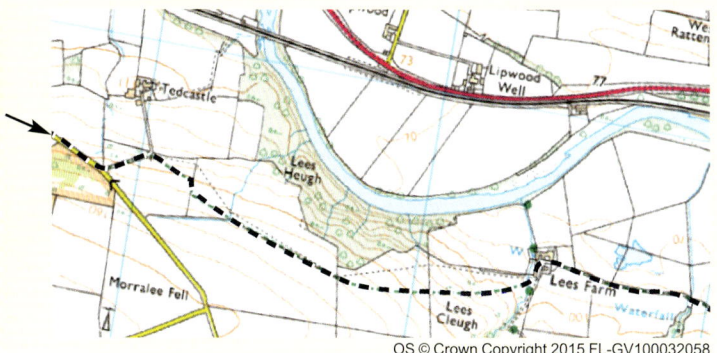

OS © Crown Copyright 2015 FL-GV100032058

At the junction bear right to follow the sign 'Plankey Mill

3; Langley 3½' and walk ahead past the entrance to the National Trust (NT) Allen Banks & Staward Gorge car park & toilets, located within the former walled garden of Ridley Hall. After about 150yds you cross a bridge over the River Allen, a tributary of the South Tyne, Here you have a choice of routes which may depend on weather conditions and time available:

Option A (entirely on road)
Continue along the road which, after bearing right, climbs steeply. After about a mile you reach an access road on the left to Tedcastle Farm. A fingerpost (at times hidden by ferns) indicates, 'Lees Farm 1; Haydon Bridge 2½'.

Option B (on permissive paths through scenic woodland with short climb on road)
After crossing the bridge over the River Allen, you need to turn immediately left. Go through the gate with a purple (National Trust) waymark and follow the path under the bridge into a field. You are now on permissive paths indicated with purple waymarks. Proceed along the field edge, with the River Allen on your right. After a RTT waymarked stile, turn immediately left and walk up the field edge. Go through a gate and turn right. Follow

Moralee Tarn

OS © Crown Copyright 2015 FL-GV100032058

the path as it bears right and begins to climb through the trees. Ignore paths off left and right. As the path levels off, you need to turn left at a RTT waymarked post.

Continue climbing steeply following the NT purple waymarks. Eventually you turn left to climb even more steeply up some stone steps. Happily you begin to descend and pass a conveniently placed bench before getting a view at a waymarked post of the Moralee Tarn. Turn left (unless you want to visit the tarn) and continue along the broad path. At the end of the tarn, ignore the waymark pointing left and instead proceed straight ahead. Just before going through a kissing gate, you pass an information panel, 'An inspiring landscape', which tells of the local artist, John Martin.

Now follow the grassy track for about 300yds to go through a further gate that leads onto a road at a small parking area. (This is the road followed by Option A.) Turn right and climb up the road for about 400yds until you reach an access road on the left to Tedcastle Farm. A fingerpost (at times hidden by ferns) indicates, 'Lees Farm 1; Haydon Bridge 2½'.

A & B

Followers of either option now proceed down the Tedcastle Farm access road for about 200yds before turning right to cross a waymarked stile by a gate. After a few yards be careful to bear right up the faint green track to cross a ladder stile in a broken wall. There is no clear path ahead but you need to make your way to the top right-hand corner of the field aiming for the gap between the woods on the left (Lees Heugh Wood) and the trees on the right. Once there, you go through the gate and after a few paces you will see the buildings of Lees Farm below. Ahead to the left, the South Tyne reappears as it winds its way to Haydon Bridge, while to the right you may be able to see the battlements of 14th-century Langley Castle (now an hotel and restaurant).

Again there is no clear path but your aim has to be towards to the far right-hand side of the buildings. Proceed down the hillside to cross a waymarked ladderstile over a stone wall. Now descend diagonally right to the right-hand side of a clump of trees. Continue down in the same direction towards the right of the farm cottages. You pass a tree on your right before you reach a fence where you need to bear right and walk a short distance to a gate in the corner where the fence meets a stone wall at a fingerpost 'Allen Banks 1'. Proceed through the gate and turn right past the farm buildings to exit onto an access road. Continue ahead for about ¾ mile to meet a minor road. Bear left and follow the road which leads under the A69 Haydon Bridge bypass.

You pass a caravan site on the left and some converted farm buildings on the right. Here, at East Land Ends, the birthplace of the artist John Martin, an information panel provides details of his early life. Continue past a variety of dwellings on the outskirts of Haydon Bridge until you reach a main road. Turn left, follow the road and then turn left just before the Anchor Hotel as Shaftoe Street becomes John Martin Street.

Cross the South Tyne over the now pedestrianised old bridge. An information panel on the bridge provides details of its chequered history. Just before the end of the bridge turn right to go down the subway steps. Before you walk through the subway, stop to enjoy the view of the river and both the old and new bridges. After you exit the subway, turn left and immediately right into Church Street where you pass a fine war memorial and St Cuthbert's Church. You then reach The Bridge (community library, visitor information point and internet café). The railway station lies a few yards ahead.

Haydon's old bridge

Haydon Bridge

Haydon Bridge has long provided an important and busy river crossing point. Little is known of an early wooden bridge nor of the origins of the stone bridge which subsequently suffered a succession of damages and repairs from the great flood of 1771 onwards. By the mid-20th century, increasing traffic led in 1960 to a temporary steel replacement until the present concrete road bridge was opened in 1970. The attractive stone bridge now continues in use for pedestrians.

The long-awaited bypass which opened in 2009 restored much needed tranquillity to this pleasant little town which straddles both sides of the South Tyne. Here you can find a range of facilities including accommodation, a library with an internet café and, of course, the railway station.

The original village of Haydon lay slightly further north of the river and is marked today by the remains of a 12th century church which bears evidence of stonework from Hadrian's Wall. There are claims that the body of St Cuthbert may have rested here earlier on its long journey from Lindisfarne to its eventual burial place in Durham in 995. Appropriately the current parish church, consecrated in 1796, bears the saint's name.

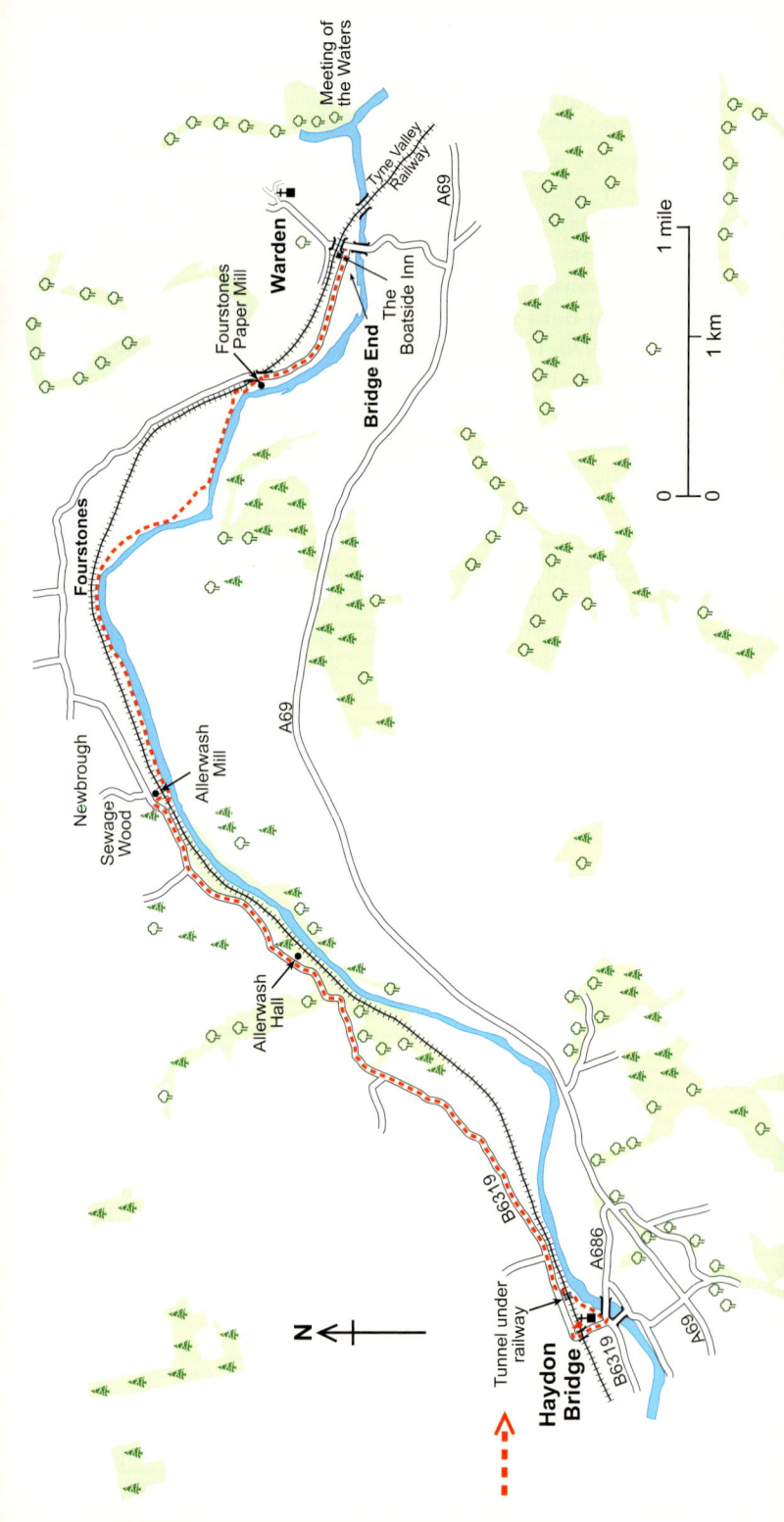

STAGE 8
Haydon Bridge to Warden
6½ miles (10.5km)

Shortly after leaving Haydon Bridge, you join a minor road which you follow for about half of this Stage. There are attractive views of the South Tyne Valley but the river itself is no longer visible for some time. You pass close to the small village of Fourstones as you walk alongside the river before the path rejoins the road for the final stretch of the walk. The Trail follows the roadside pavement to Warden, where the North and South Tyne routes converge very conveniently at the popular Boatside Inn. With this stage being relatively short you may wish to combine it with a further stage. Conveniently, Hexham, with train, bus and taxi links, lies only 2½ miles further ahead.

Entry/exit points	Haydon Bridge (GR843645); Warden 6½ miles (10.5km)
Map	OS Explorer OL43 Hadrian's Wall
Refreshments	Pubs and The Bridge internet café in Haydon Bridge; The Boatside Inn at Warden

The Walk
From Haydon Bridge Station walk down Church Street past The Bridge (community library, visitor information point and internet café) and St Cuthbert's Church to the T-junction. Turn left and after 20yds turn left again. A fingerpost on the right, sometimes partially hidden by foliage, directs you to Station Road (B6319). You pass a picnic area as you walk along the surfaced path which takes you close to the railway line on the embankment above. After a couple of hundred yards, the

Leaving Haydon Bridge

path leads under the railway line and you turn right onto the road (B 6319).

You will be walking for about 3 miles on this normally quiet road. However, without a footpath and little in the way of grass verges, due care needs to be taken. Initially the road climbs steadily before becoming more undulating. The road winds through a wooded area and after about 2 miles a sign indicates that you are at Allerwash. On your right you pass the high walls of Allerwash Hall which has its own short section of pavement.

You proceed past a collection of cottages and farm buildings as well as a road (Church Lane) on the left from Newbrough. The road descends and crosses the Newbrough Burn shortly after which there is a parking place on the

South Tyne reappears

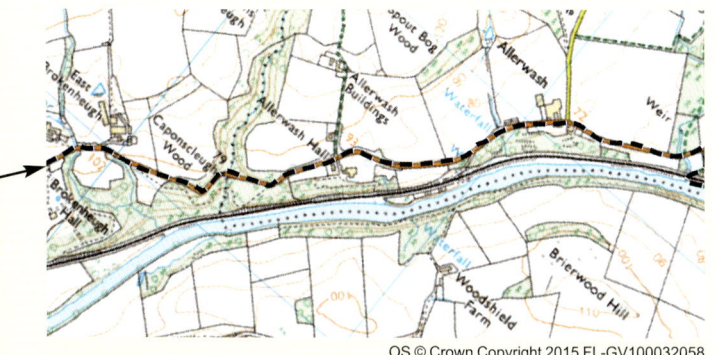

right. Here turn right at the fingerpost 'Fourstones 1; Warden Bridge End 3'. Follow the path as it goes to the right of the property (Allerwash Mill), ignore the metal gate on the left and go down the steps towards the Newbrough Burn. Turn left to go under the bridge and there at last is the South Tyne again!

Turn left to clamber over the stones to join a narrow path running alongside the river. Proceed along the path for a couple of hundred yards or so. Just after a clump of trees go through the gap in the wall on your left, turn right and continue in the same direction. This avoids an eroded part of the riverside path. You can either continue on this green path or soon after passing under telephone wires, you can bear right to rejoin the parallel riverside path and proceed downstream. Eventually, both the green path and the riverside path converge and you walk past a cottage and some old farm buildings as you carry on to the right of a waymarked gate.

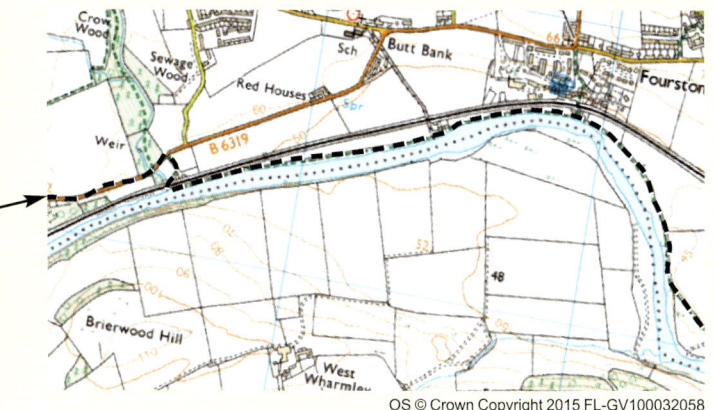

Fine stretch

When you reach a large house, ignore the track off to the left and walk respectfully over the grass to the right of the building. Continue ahead with a fence on your left for about ½ mile. The path is then diverted a little further away from the river through a kissing gate. The path narrows and leads over a rather high stile. It's not long before you are walking once more alongside the river. Care is needed as the path is narrow and uneven and the bank is steep in parts. Eventually you emerge back onto the road.

Turn right and walk along the pavement to pass the Fourstones Paper Mill complex. The company has been making specialist paper since 1763! Proceed down the, at times, busy road for about three-quarters of a mile, making

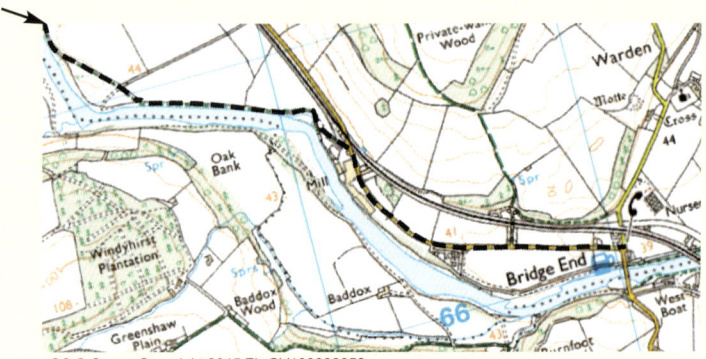

OS © Crown Copyright 2015 FL-GV100032058

Routes converge

judicious use of the available pavements to arrive at the popular Boatside Inn at Bridge End, Warden. Here your route converges with the route from the source of the North Tyne.

Waters Meet Option

However, unless you are in a hurry, you have the opportunity to add an extra mile in order to view the confluence of the North and South Tyne at the beginning of the journey of the River Tyne itself to the sea. On the left, looking at the bridge from the front of The Boatside Inn, a fingerpost indicates, 'Waters Meet ½'. Follow the path past Bridge End Cottage. Some stone steps take you to the riverside, turn left and follow the path to 'Junction Pool Bench', where you can sit and admire the confluence of the three Rivers Tyne. Now retrace your steps back to The Boatside Inn where you may like to enjoy some refreshments.

Meeeting at Waters Meet

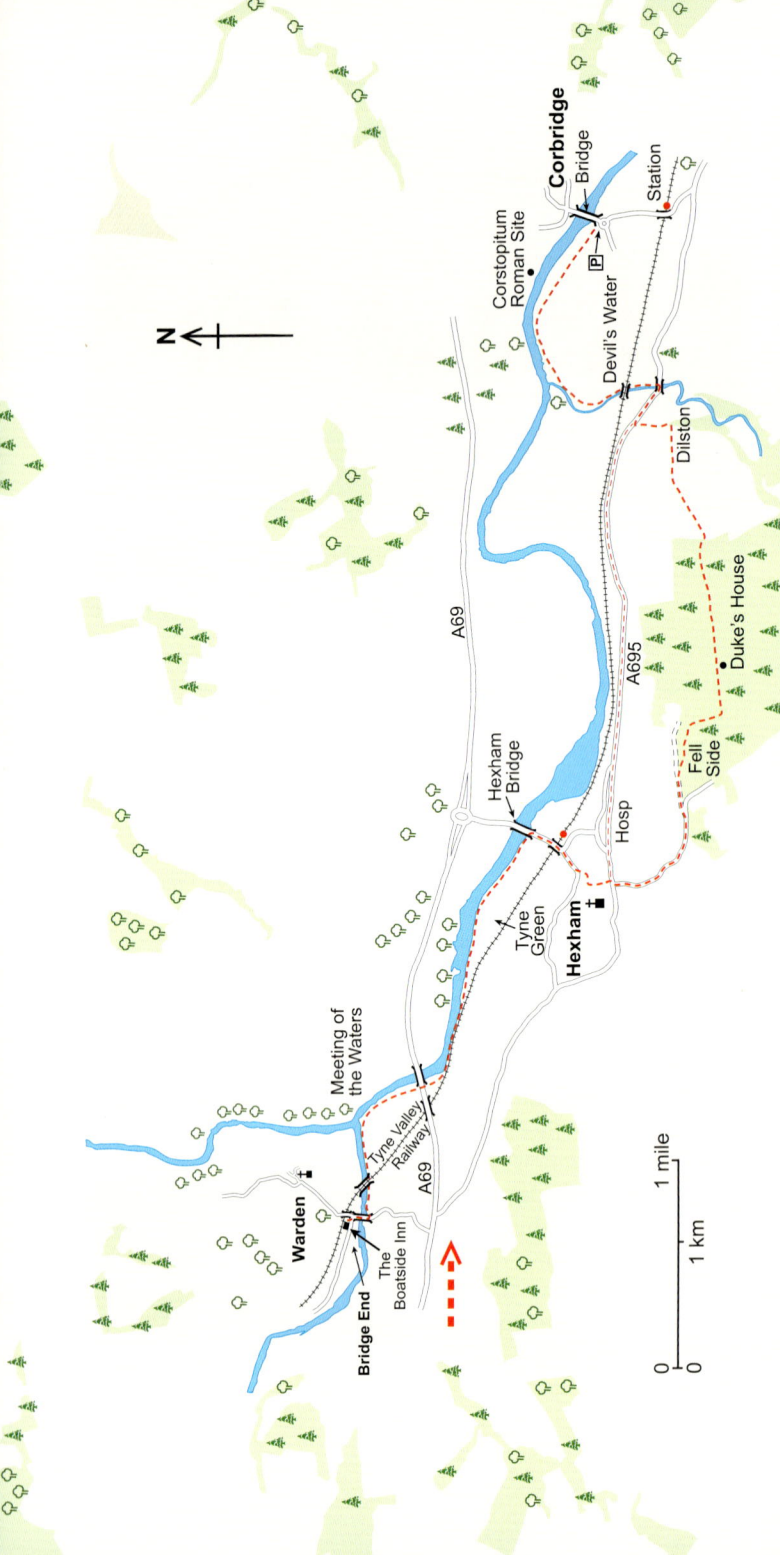

STAGE 9
Warden to Corbridge
7½ miles (12.1km)

The north and south routes having converged at Bridge End, Warden, the Trail now follows the South Tyne for a short distance to its meeting with its counterpart, the North Tyne. You then follow the River Tyne proper along the riverbank to Hexham. There is not a right of way along the riverside immediately to the east of Hexham, so the Trail needs to continue inland into the centre of Hexham with its abbey and amenities. There is a fairly steep climb for about ½ mile out of Hexham before you set off on a pleasant countryside walk largely through woodland. The Trail then descends to Dilston. Walkers who are pressed for time and/or if the weather conditions are poor, have the option of using a roadside path for the section from Hexham to Dilston (see below). From Dilston, you are on a pleasant path all the way to Corbridge.

Entry/exit points	Bridge End, Warden (GR910660); Hexham 2¾ miles (4.4km); Dilston 6½ miles (10.5km); Corbridge 7½ miles (12.1km)
Map	OS Explorer OL43 Hadrian's Wall
Refreshments	Inn at Warden; cafés and pubs at Hexham and Corbridge

The walk

From The Boatside Inn, Bridge End, Warden, walk across the bridge to the old Toll House. Turn left and cross the road onto an access road in the direction of the sign 'Hexham 2; Cycleway 72'. If you are not happy with narrow and uneven paths you could walk straight ahead along the Cycleway 72 until you converge with the riverside route at point (**A**) below. Otherwise, however, to follow the riverside, after about 175yds turn left at the entrance drive to the first property, Ferrymans Cottage. Walk to the right of the large

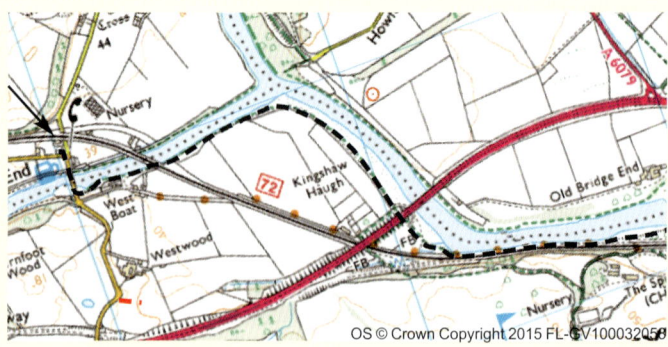

wooden gates to pick up a path that leads towards the river where you turn right.

Continue ahead on the riverside path passing under the railway bridge. Care needs to be taken as the path becomes somewhat narrower and gets close to the steep bankside. At a fork, bear right to climb up the clearer path. Now look out on your right for the Daft as a Brush stone marking the meeting of the waters. Continue ahead as you now follow the River Tyne at the start of its journey to the sea. After passing beneath the A69 road bridge, continue along the riverside. You cross a short footbridge over a stream. As the path forks, continue ahead on the broader path and climb the steps and turn left to join the surfaced cycle route path parallel to the railway (**A**). Follow the surfaced path to a gate

Brian Burnie at the marker stone

Tyne Green

at a railway crossing. Just before the gate, turn left, then bear right. Follow the path nearest to the riverside through Tyne Green Country Park with Tynedale Golf Course on the right. Hexham Bridge (1793) comes into sight. Eventually, with the boathouses on your right, turn right just before the bridge and then bear left to make your way to the main road.

Turn right and follow the pavement into Hexham, going over the railway bridge and passing a mini-roundabout (the

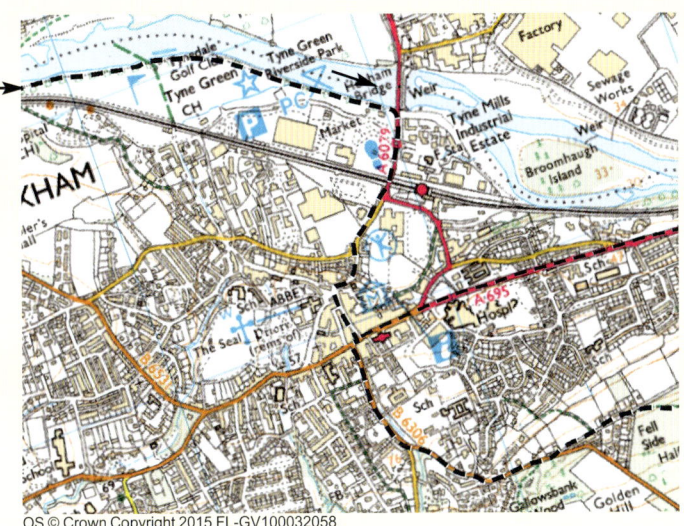

Hexham Abbey (*Photograph: Graeme Peacock*)

Hexham
Historically, the development of the town has been closely interwoven with that of the abbey. The abbey today with its refectory café and gift shop stands, rather like a spiritual oasis, in the centre of the town, surrounded by pleasant grounds, bustling streets and a market place. Hexham has a variety of shopping and leisure facilities and good rail and public transport links. The Tourist Information Office, public toilets, car and railway station, can be found through the Gatehouse.

station lies to the left) to arrive at some pedestrian lights. Cross over to the other side of the road and turn right. Now follow the pavement as it climbs steeply. At the top of Hallstile Bank, turn left into the Market Place and there on the right is Hexham Abbey. On your left is the historic Gatehouse or Moot Hall.

To continue, walk up pedestrianised Fore Street and just before the HSBC bank, bear right to meet the main road (A695). Here you have a choice of routes:

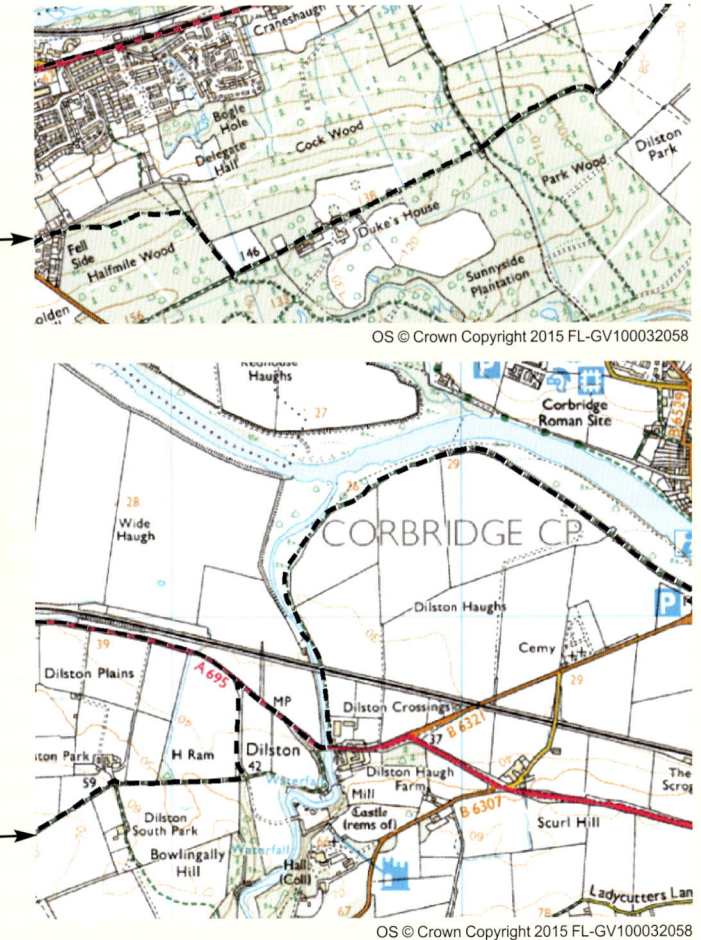

OS © Crown Copyright 2015 FL-GV100032058

Option A (roadside path)
If you are pressed for time and/or it has been very wet you may prefer to walk along the roadside path to Dilston. In this case turn left and follow the A695 Corbridge road for 2½ miles to Dilston Bridge, see **A & B** below, saving ½ mile.

Option B (cross country with climbs and views)
Turn right at the main road and then use the pedestrian lights to cross to the other side. Turn left and after a few yards turn right to walk up Eastgate. When convenient cross the road and continue on the left-hand side pavement. After about ¼ mile, bear left at the fork in the road to continue on the B6306, climbing for a about a further ¼ mile to arrive

Devils Water meets the Tyne

at Fellside. Turn left along the access road, passing a pleasant row of cottages with views over the town. On the right, some 10yds beyond a vehicle turning circle at the remains of an old quarry, take the public footpath 'Dukes House ¾'.

Follow the narrow path as it undulates quite steeply at times and eventually broadens and becomes stony before levelling off to pass a clearing and reach an access road. Turn left in the direction 'Dilston 1½' and follow the broad tree-lined track which passes Duke's House with its ornate chimney pots. The current property is a refurbished Victorian house said to have been built on the site of a house belonging to the Duke of Portland.

The access road becomes a narrow, and at times, an uneven path. Ignore paths off. At the end of the wood, follow the path as it bears left, with a field on the right and a further field on the left beyond the bushes. The narrow path descends to an access track. Cross over and continue ahead on what is now a broader path to reach a road. Cross over the road, go through a gate. On your right is Dilston Scout Camp and on your left you then pass Dilston Physic Garden. You meet a further access road at a former mill, now a B&B, beyond which runs a river, known as 'Devils Water', which will soon accompany you as it flows to join the Tyne.

Turn left to walk a short distance to the main road (A695) which you need to cross with great care. Turn right and walk across Dilston Bridge (the alternative road walk from Hexham joins here).

A & B

At the end of the bridge, turn immediately left at the public footpath sign 'Corbridge 1¾'. Follow the path with Devils Water on your left to some steps that climb to a gate at the side of the railway. Take extreme care to cross over the railway lines. Continue ahead on the clear path which bears right to join an embankment. Further on the left Devils Water converges with the River Tyne. You now follow the embankment for about a mile to Corbridge.

Just before the bridge (the only Tyne bridge to survive the great flood of 1771), leave the embankment and go through a gate to meet a road at the south end of the bridge (there is a convenient car park to the right). The village centre lies over the bridge. The starting point of Stage 10 of the Trail

Corbridge (*Photograph: Graeme Peacock*)

is on the opposite side of the road at the Lion Court apartments. (There is a one way system for traffic on the bridge, so use the traffic lights to cross the road.) However, this stage now ends here.

Corbridge (*Photograph: Graeme Peacock*)

Corbridge
A visit to the centre of Corbridge, situated at the north end of Corbridge Bridge, enables you to enjoy the attractions of this fascinating village. The bridge itself dates from 1674 and was the only Tyne bridge not destroyed by the terrible flood of 1771.

Corbridge has a market place and this is dominated by the parish church of St Andrew, "which is the most important surviving Saxon monument in Northumberland, except for Hexham crypt" (Pevsner, 1992). It is possible that the Saxon builders made use of stones from the nearby Roman great camp of Corstopitum. Corstopitum also provided a convenient source of material for other buildings, including the 14th century Vicar's Pele, built in the churchyard as a defence against Scots' incursions. The site can be visited a short distance west of Corbridge.

Today, these and other historic features, as well as its various eating places and traditional and boutique shops, have contributed to the popularity of the village as a place to visit. It is also seen as an attractive place to live. Its location, 18 miles from Newcastle, and road and rail improvements, means that many residents now commute to work in the Newcastle and Gateshead conurbation. It has also become a fashionable place for retired people to live. The railway station lies about ½ mile south of the bridge.

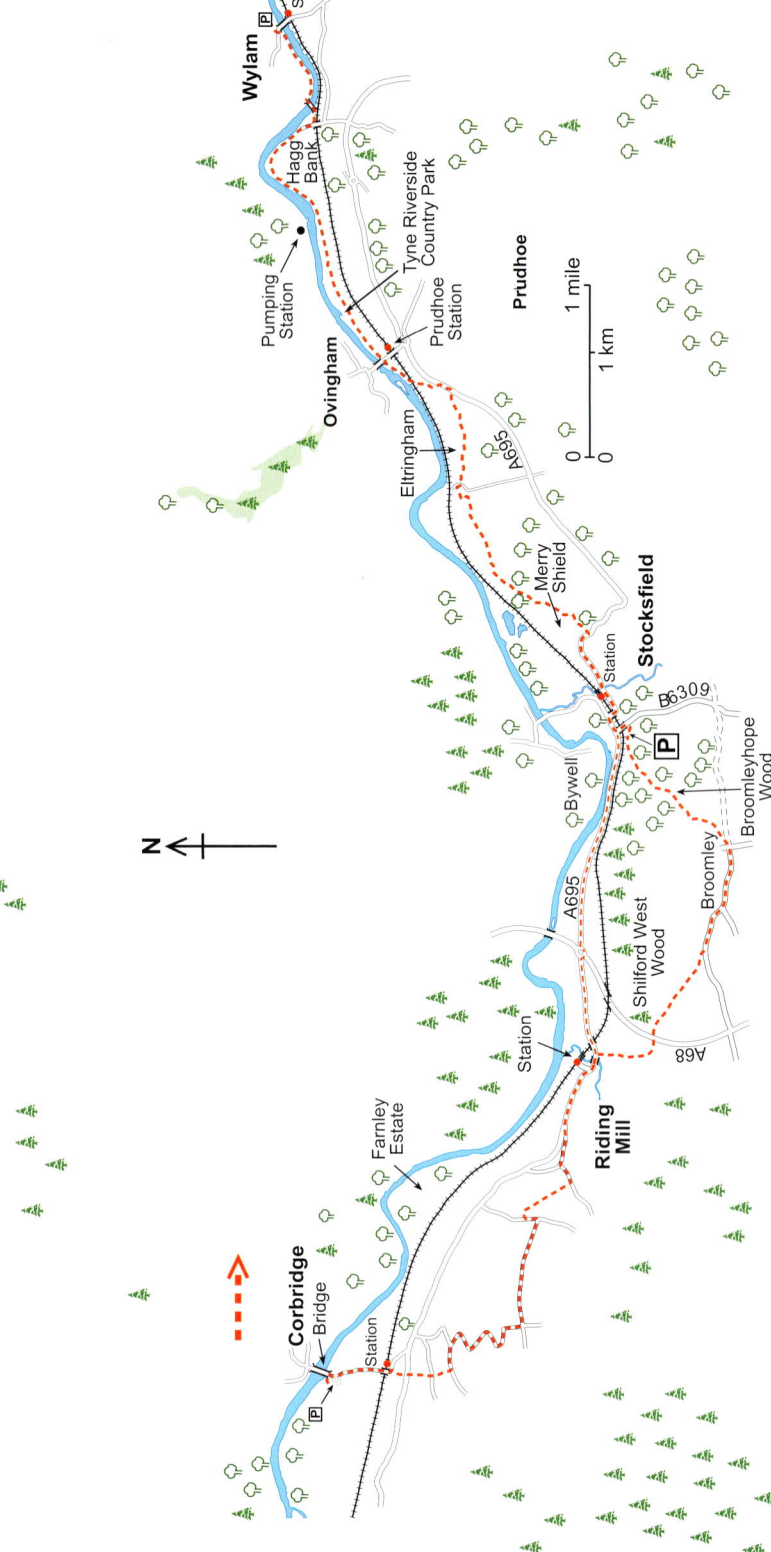

STAGE 10
Corbridge to Wylam
13¼ miles (21.2km)

This stage of the Trail closely follows the Tyne most of the way on pleasant undulating green paths. Unfortunately, part of the riverside path from Corbridge to Riding Mill has remained closed following a landslide in 2015. At the time of writing this had not been reopened, hence the route remains diverted inland. However, check the DAAB website for updates. After Riding Mill, the Trail climbs through some delightful woodland and crosses some farmland before descending towards Stocksfield. If time is pressing and the weather conditions are unfavourable, there is the alternative of a more direct route along a roadside path.

Entry/exit points	Corbridge (GR989641); Riding Mill 3 miles (4.8km); Stocksfield 6 miles (9.6km); Prudhoe 9 miles (14.4km); Wylam 13¼ miles (21.2km)
Maps	OS Explorer OL43 Hadrian's Wall; OS Explorer 316 Newcastle upon Tyne
Refreshments	Cafés and pubs in Corbridge; hotel in Riding Mill; riverside café at Prudhoe; pubs & tearoom in Wylam

The walk

This stage begins from Corbridge at the south end of the bridge at the access road in front of the Lion Court apartments. Turn right and follow the access road as it joins a more main road (Station Road). Continue straight ahead, on the right-hand side pavement when convenient, as the road climbs to go over the railway bridge. Just beyond the two traffic mirrors, go up the steps to enter the woods. Bear right and follow the path between the trees and go through the waymarked gate. Continue up the field edge. At the top of the field go over the stile. Cross the road with care and enter the field opposite. Continue along the field edge with shrub land on your right. Leave the field by the waymarked

OS © Crown Copyright 2015 FL-GV100032058

stile. Cross the lane (Ladycutter Lane) and go through the waymarked gate. Continue straight ahead, climbing quite steeply at times as you pass through further kissing gates to meet an access road at Mount Pleasant Cottage.

Turn left and walk down the road for a short way and bear right at the fork. Proceed up the road bearing right at the access road to Burn Brae Lodge.

In the woods

Continue along the minor road as it climbs steadily with woods on your left before it bears left to climb past High Ash and High Level Cottage. At the top of the climb you pass Prospect Hill farm. At the crossroads be sure to turn left. The road descends gradually for about ¾ mile. At the T-junction turn left. After about 220yds, turn right to leave the road at a fingerpost and walk down the side of a field, on the left of which is a property at Riding Hills. Turn right at the field corner and walk along the field edge with the hedge on your left. Continue as the field boundary turns left and walk downhill. You pass through two gates before arriving at a road. Turn left and follow this slightly busier road past the pleasant properties of Beauclerc. Continue along the road as it bears right and descends to meet the main road (A695). Cross over with care and turn right to descend into Riding Mill. You pass a road (Dene Terrace) on the left leading to the railway station before arriving at The

Wellington (hotel, bar and restaurant). Continue ahead for a short distance.

You soon see a junction on your right. Here you have a choice of routes:

Option A (roadside path)

If time is pressing and/or the weather is bad, you may prefer to continue straight ahead along the roadside path for the next 2 miles – saving a mile but missing some delightful countryside. After leaving Riding Mill, cross over to the other side of the road when convenient to continue along the right-hand pavement and the green path. Take care to pass the roundabout at the junction with the A68. At a layby you need to cross to the other side of the road and pick up the roadside path again. Eventually the main route emerges on the right from the B6308 Ebchester road to join the roadside path – now continue from **A & B** below.

Riding Mill

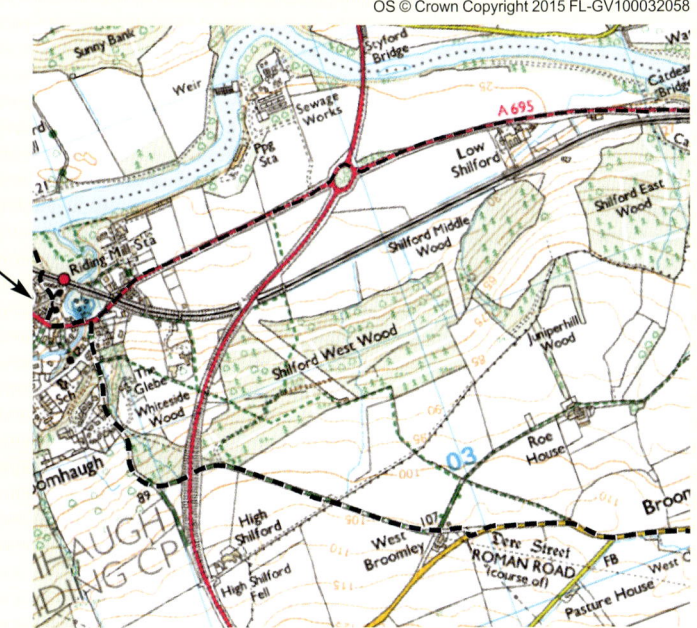

OS © Crown Copyright 2015 FL-GV100032058

OS © Crown Copyright 2015 FL-GV100032058

Option B (cross-country route)

At the junction you need to cross over the main road with care to walk up Whiteside Bank. After about 100yds turn left, immediately past Whiteside Cottage, at the fingerpost, 'Broomley 1¼'. The narrow path climbs steeply. You cross a waymarked stile. Walk diagonally right across the field, on the faint path, towards the right-hand side of the property just visible between the trees (Wentworth Grange Nursing and Residential Care Home). Continue on the path as it bears left past the property to a kissing gate in the fence. Go through the gate and climb up the steps to reach the main road (A68). Take extremely great care to cross this busy road.

A fingerpost suggests that Broomley is now 1½ miles away (and it may be even a little further!). Proceed ahead, go through the kissing gate and walk between the paddock fences. Go over the waymarked stile and enter the woods. You will find that the route is generally well waymarked from now onwards. Walk ahead, cross a vehicular track and continue to climb steadily. At a T-junction of paths, turn left and follow the now more level path. At another T-junction, turn right to resume climbing again with a fence on your left. The path leads past a stone-cladded pumping station on your left and you arrive at a stile at the edge of the woods.

Cross the stile, turn left and proceed ahead along the edge of the field. A small plank-crossing leads into a second field. Continue ahead to walk around the edge of two sides of the field until you meet a broad track with a gateway in the wall directly ahead. Go through the gateway and continue ahead along the field-edge path with a wire fence on your left. Exit the field at the top left-hand corner through a narrow opening to meet a minor road with a fingerpost on your right. Cross over the minor road and go over the stile. Continue ahead with the fence on your left. At the end of the field, go over the ladder stile to arrive at a road. Cross to the other side of the road and turn left. You now need to walk along the road for about 500yds taking due care as you may encounter large vehicles. The road takes you through the neat hamlet of Broomley.

As the road bears right at a junction, take care to cross straight over to join a broad public byway. Walk about 40yds and turn left to go through a gate by the fingerpost 'Stocksfield 1¼'. Bear diagonally right as indicated by the fingerpost and walk towards the power-line post with a pond over to your right. The faint green path continues towards the left hand-side corner of the field before descending to cross a small footbridge over the Smithy Burn. Climb to go through a gate and follow the path with a fence on your right and the burn below on the left. Turn right at a waymark as the path leaves the burn, and after 20yds bear left at a fork onto the clearer path between the trees. After about 75yds, at a T-junction, turn left and continue on the broad path through the ancient woodland.

You meet a fingerpost 'Stocksfield 1' where you follow the path as it bears left. The path leads across a dip which can be particularly muddy. Continue straight ahead. Ignore paths off as the path narrows and you descend through a clearing. Eventually the path leads to a small car park which you enter past a metal barrier or through a gap in the right-hand side hedge. Proceed through the car park, turn left on the minor road (B6309 Ebchester) and go over the railway bridge to meet a road (A695). Cross the busy road with care to join the pavement and turn right.

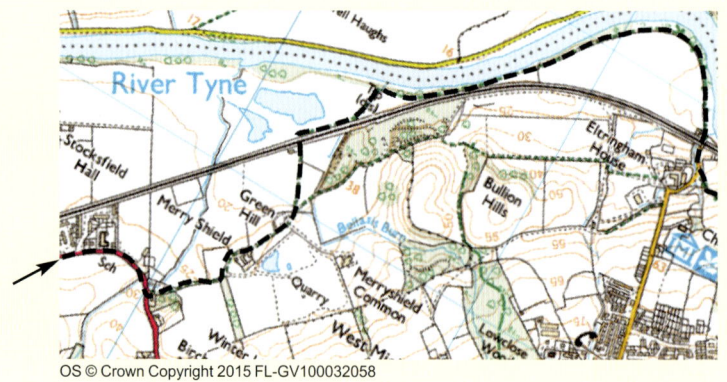

OS © Crown Copyright 2015 FL-GV100032058

A & B

The alternative route from Riding Mill along the roadside converges with the main route at this point.

Continue ahead, ignoring the road on the left to Bywell, and proceed through Stocksfield. Soon after the railway station, you are in more open country. Almost immediately after passing the entrance to Stocksfield Sports Fields, make sure to turn left onto a lane (5mph sign). Ignore paths off and carry on past the farm buildings (Merry Shield). There are traces of a quarry on the right. Go through a waymarked gate and through the tunnel under the railway line. Turn right and walk ahead. There is a large pond to the left. Follow the line of the field boundary on the right along two sides of the field until you arrive at a metal gate. Go through the gate, down the steps and across the footbridge to a waymark. Carry on with the river once again nearby as you pass through the fishing area (Eltringham Fishings).

Eventually you arrive at a railway crossing. Observe the instructions to cross the railway with very careful attention to the warning lights. Proceed uphill. At a crossing of paths turn left at the sign 'Restricted Byway Eltringham ½'. The path climbs steeply and you pass a pleasant property. Continue ahead ignoring a sign to Prudhoe on the right. The path exits onto an access road. Turn right and then left at the factory to follow the narrow path alongside the factory railings with the bushes and the road to your right.

At the end of the industrial plant turn left at the public footpath sign 'Tyne Riverside Park ¼'. Proceed down, with the metal railings on your left, and follow the path as it descends towards the river. After passing a Woodland Trust sign, fork left then bear right on the main track. You reach

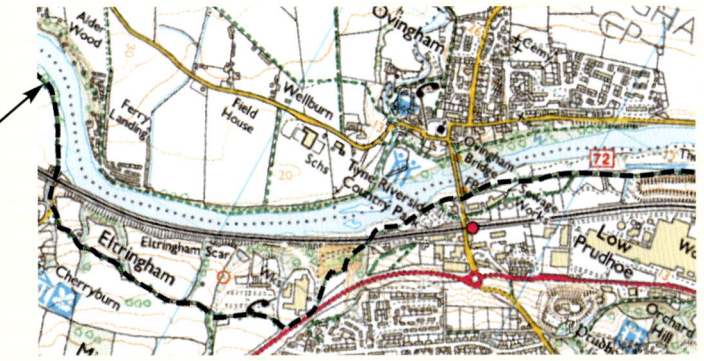

OS © Crown Copyright 2015 FL-GV100032058

the railway line. Cross the line with the usual great care. Bear immediately left on a grassy path towards the river. Follow the path, with the river on your left to reach an entrance to the Tyne Riverside Country Park car park. The Trail carries straight on. However, depending on season/time, refreshments maybe available at the Tyne Riverside Café, next to the car park. Prudhoe Station lies to the right of the café.

To continue on the Trail, walk ahead on the surfaced track under the motor bridge and the adjacent footbridge. The track is popular with cyclists and you may prefer to walk closer to the river. If so, after about 200yds, as the surfaced track bears right, leave the track and bear left towards the

Prudhoe Bridge in sight

Pumping Station

riverside. Here, you will pick up a narrow but well-trodden path. Now make your way ahead along the riverside for several hundred yards. After a small footbridge you come close to the surfaced track again but unless the conditions are muddy, bear left and continue closer to the river. Eventually, the narrow riverside path bears right and you rejoin the surfaced track.

Continue ahead along the track. On the other side of the river, you will see a prominent tower, part of the 19th-century Wylam Pumping Station. The Trail climbs quite steeply. As the track descends, you pass some fine property and go through a paddock area. Carry on until you arrive at the foot of Hagg Bank and a sign for Cycleway 72. However, don't proceed up the bank but instead leave the main track and fork left. Walk along the clear path which returns

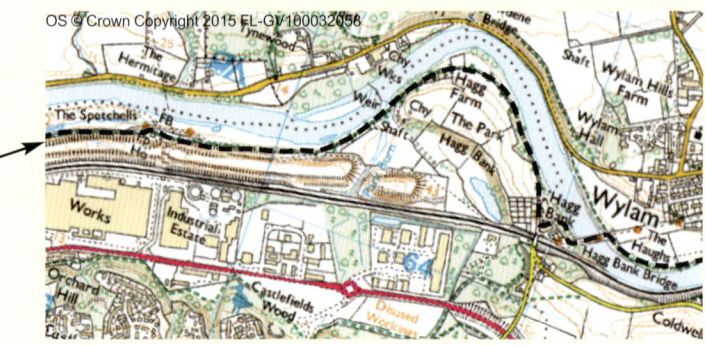

OS © Crown Copyright 2015 FL-GV100032058

towards the riverside. Follow the path, which can be narrow and steeply cambered in parts, until it climbs to arrive at Hagg Bank Bridge.

Turn left and cross this delightful bridge (an information panel at the far end provides details). Once over the bridge, turn immediately right down the steps back to the riverside. Proceed ahead, ignoring paths off, until the path turns sharp left to pass some allotments. Follow the path as it climbs to a junction then bear right to arrive at the cricket field. Turn right and take the path back into the woods.

Turn left to walk with the fence and the sports field on your left. Continue straight ahead past a terrace of houses and go down some steps for the final section along the

Hagg Bank Bridge (*Photograph: Graeme Peacock*)

Nearing Wylam

riverside. The path leads under Wylam Bridge (1836) and you climb to an access road where you turn left. (The main road leads on the left across the bridge to Wylam Station and the Boathouse pub, while to the right, it leads to the village and its amenities.) Follow the access road passing the war memorial on your left. Turn right into the Tyne Riverside Country Park car park and walk ahead to some information panels, 'Wylam Car Park' and the end of this stage

> ### Wylam
> The small, pretty village of Wylam is now a pleasant place to live, with easy commuting to NewcastleGateshead. This contrasts with its industrial past when it was heavily involved in the extraction of coal and iron, being described by one late Victorian commentator as the very worst colliery village he had seen. Wylam Station is one of the oldest stations still in use. The former station master's house (1835) is a listed building; a plaque commemorates William Hedley, who attended school here and is famous as the inventor of the locomotive Puffing Billy. George Stephenson, sometimes called the "father of the railways" and Timothy Hackforth, an engineer, were born here and carried out pioneering work in the development of steam locomotion.
>
> On the walk we crossed the Wylam Railway Bridge of 1876 (Hagg Bank Bridge), now disused but pedestrianised, which

provided a link with the Newcastle to Carlisle railway; its single-span arch is reminiscent of Newcastle's Tyne Bridge. Later, on the next stage, we pass the humble cottage where George Stephenson was born. It is owned by the National Trust and is open to the public.

Wylam War Memorial

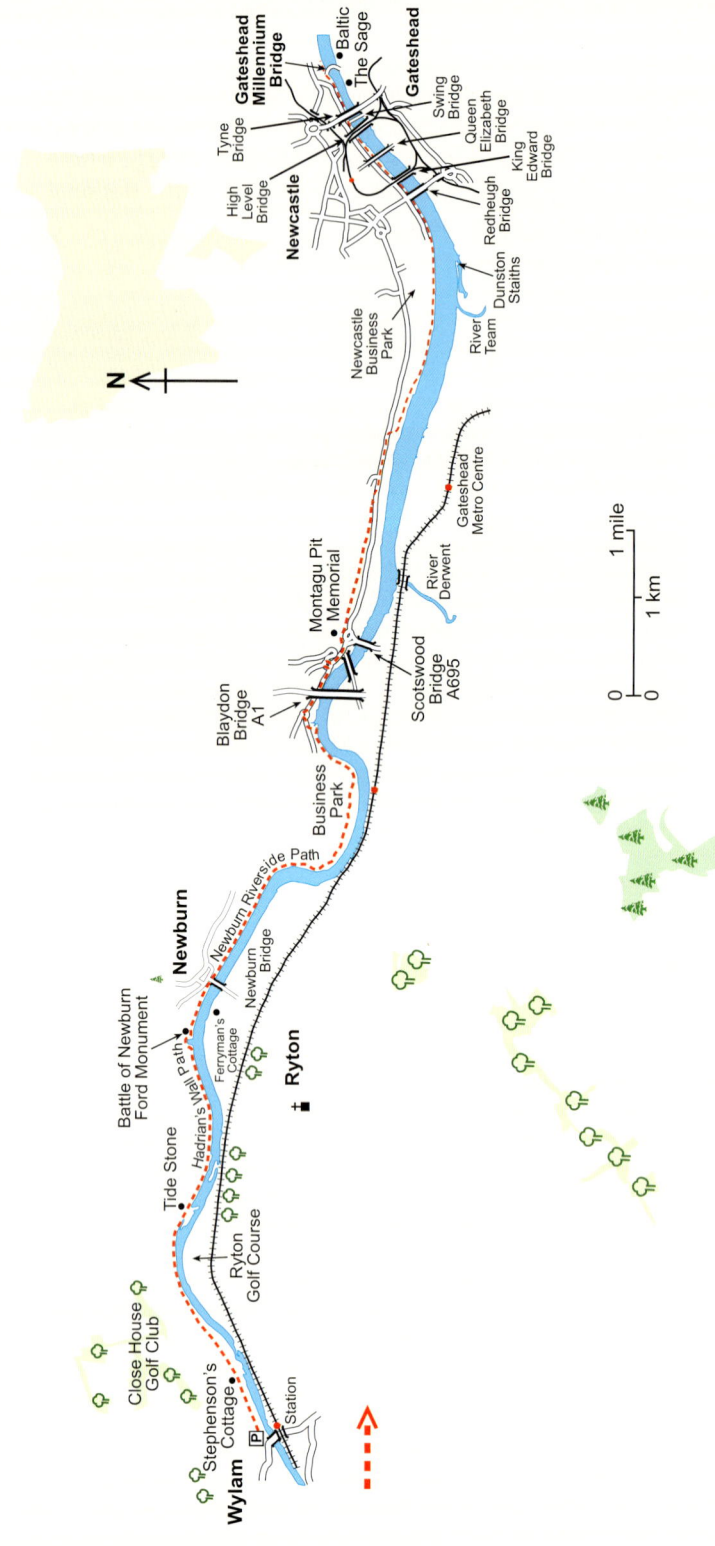

STAGE 11
Wylam to NewcastleGateshead
10½ miles (16.9km)

The Trail now begins to approach urban Tyneside. It commences with a delightful stroll along the riverside from Wylam to Newburn. You pass the birthplace of the famous railway engineer, George Stephenson. From Newburn onwards the Trail is on surfaced paths almost entirely close to the river which, since leaving Wylam, has become tidal. There is clear evidence of regeneration where former power stations and industrial sites have been replaced by office buildings and modern housing. You will be reminded of the importance of William (Lord) Armstrong to the industrial heritage of Tyneside before you arrive at Newcastle Quayside and the iconic Gateshead Millennium Bridge.

Entry/exit points	**Wylam (GR112643); Newburn 3¼ miles (5.2km); Newcastle Quayside 10½ miles (16.9km)**
Map	**OS Explorer 316 Newcastle upon Tyne**
Refreshments	**Pubs and tearoom in Wylam; riverside café and pubs at Newburn; cafés in Newburn Industrial Estate and Newburn Riverside, pubs and cafés on Newcastle and Gateshead Quaysides**

The walk
The walk starts at the information panels 'Wylam Car Park' on the site of the former North Wylam Station (1876-1968). Turn right in the direction of Newburn, pass through a gateway and cross an access road to walk along the mid-18th century waggonway. After about ½ mile you reach the birthplace of the noted railway engineer George Stephenson (1781-1848). The cottage is a National Trust property and, together with its café, is open to visitors at regular times as indicated on the noticeboard. From here you have a choice of routes:

Option A
(along the shared path on the former waggonway)

To proceed head on the broad track until eventually you arrive at a junction where you need to turn right to continue on the NCN72. After a row of cottages, you go through a gate and bear

From Wylam Bridge

left to reach a further junction where a signpost indicates one more mile to Newburn and the acorn symbol tells you that you are joining a National Trail ('Hadrians Path').

Option B (along a narrow riverside path which is subject to erosion)

Opposite Stephenson's Cottage, go through the kissing gate and walk a short distance to go through a further kissing gate in the fence on your left. You have now joined the pleasant riverside path roughly parallel to the waggonway that leads ahead to Newburn. After a further 200yds or so, you come to an open space where the path forks. Take the left-hand fork and follow the grassy path which leads between trees. From here onwards, ignore paths off to the left unless you wish to return to the nearby waggonway in case of inclement weather or the need to make haste. At a junction of paths keep straight ahead close to the fence on your left. At times,

Riverside path

OS © Crown Copyright 2015 FL-GV100032058

Chance to rest

Close House Golf Course and the football and rugby pitches used by Newcastle University can be seen beyond the waggonway.

Eventually the narrow path veers right to reach a well-trodden path that goes along the right-hand edge of a field. At the end of the field you enter a wooded area. As the path descends look out for a wooden fence on your left, in front of which there is an old stone marker, the Tide Stone. You can just make out the date, 1785, and the three-castles emblem of Newcastle Corporation. The stone indicated the town boundary at that time, as well as the point at which the Tyne was tidal until dredging moved the limit further upstream nearer to Wylam around 1900.

OS © Crown Copyright 2015 FL-GV100032058

Newburn riverside

Continue ahead on the tree-lined riverside path with a wire fence and a field on your left. Eventually, towards the end of the field, bear left and follow the path as it climbs to a kissing gate. Go through the gate, and continue along a surfaced path to a junction where a signpost indicates one more mile to Newburn, while the acorn symbol tells you that you are joining a National Trail ('Hadrians Path').

A & B
Followers of either option now proceed ahead parallel to the river. Eventually, you pass a pleasant green space with

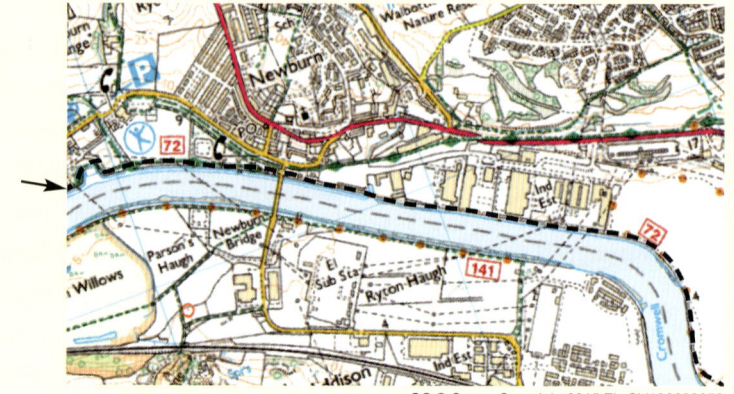

OS © Crown Copyright 2015 FL-GV100032058

picnic benches. The river bears right and Newburn Bridge comes into sight. You pass a children's play area and the path bears left at a large concrete sculpture. Turn right to pass the top of the slipway, unless you wish to seek nourishment in Hedley's Riverside Café Shop or The Keelman pub along the access road to the left of the café.

The path continues around a car park, beyond which is a monument to the Battle of Newburn Ford of 1640. Several information panels provide details. The path makes its way across a small footbridge as the Reigh Burn enters the Tyne. Turn right along the path until you reach and continue along an access road. You pass the Tyne Amateur Rowing Club (1852). On the opposite bank is Tyne United Rowing Club and, beyond the bridge, Newcastle University Rowing Club. The strong presence of these clubs serves as reminder of the historical importance of rowing on the Tyne. You pass The Boathouse, now Branzino Restaurant, where, to the left of the entrance, there is a plaque with further information about George Stephenson, while, to the right, markings on the wall indicate some dramatic flood heights of the Tyne, particularly that of the Great Flood of 1771.

You arrive at some traffic lights at Newburn Bridge (Newburn, with its amenities and bus services, lies to the left). Take great care to cross the road, proceed ahead a few yards and bear left to join Hadrian's Way, Cycleway 72. Continue on the surfaced path for about 350yds before bearing right down a narrow path down to a road (Shelley Road). Turn left and continue along the pavement through Newburn Industrial Estate with its variety of business units including refreshments facilities. At the end of the road, turn right at the sign 'Newburn Riverside ½; Newcastle

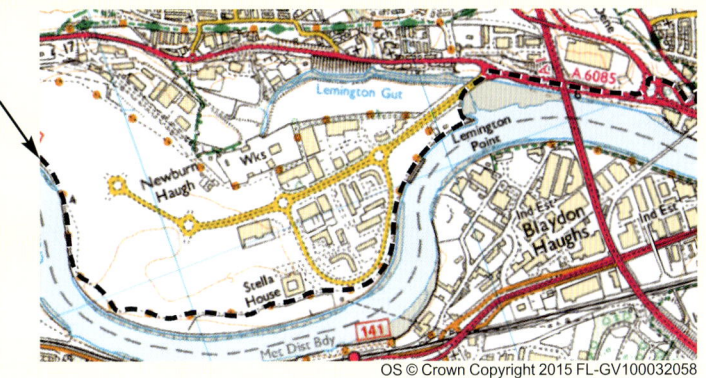

OS © Crown Copyright 2015 FL-GV100032058

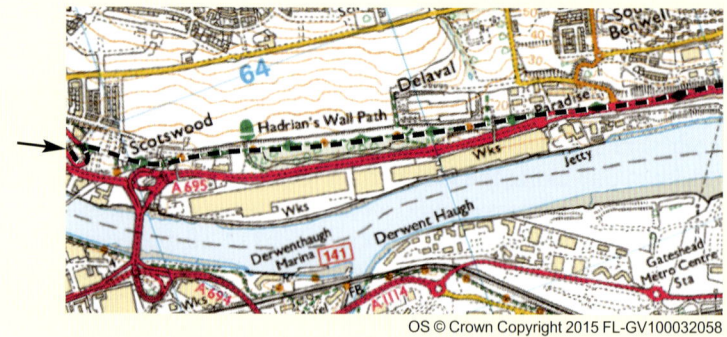

Quayside 5'. Walk along the path and you soon return to a wide expanse of river opposite a modern housing estate. Now simply keep to the broad surfaced riverside path as you proceed through Newburn Riverside Park.

Continue ahead on the riverside path. Below on the right is a small marina at Lemington Gut. You arrive at the main access road to what is Newburn Business Park. Turn right and walk ahead. You cross Lemington Bridge with its ornate white lampposts. Bear right and join the riverside path. Continuing ahead, you reach a set of traffic lights at an access road. Turn right to walk a short distance along the riverside path to the entrance to Enterprise rent-a-car. Turn left up the narrow path and turn right. After a few yards, at the NCN72 sign, use the pedestrian lights to cross the busy dual carriageway. Turn right and after some 150yds bear left to climb up the path on the Hadrian's Cycleway.

At the top of the rise, ignore a path off to the left but stop and look back over the grassy area to the left where you may be able to see a sculpture of white figures and a horse. This monument is a poignant reminder that coalfields were

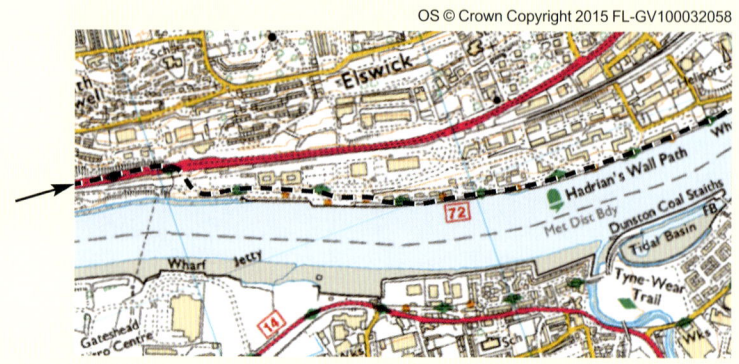

worked in this area until the late 1950s and it commemorates the death of thirty-eight miners at the Montagu View Pit in 1925.

Walk ahead and at a fork bear left to continue along Hadrian's Way. Keep on the broad path. You are walking on land reclaimed from the crowded terraces that once ran towards the industries that lined Scotswood Road. On your right, you pass some remains of the abutments of the railway that once ran along here. Through the trees to the right, you may see a factory building, currently the engineering Reece Group. However, for over 150 years, it had been part of the site of the engineering firm founded by William (later Lord) Armstrong (see below). Continue along the path which eventually descends to a main road (Scotswood Road). Continue ahead on the shared pavement and then use the traffic lights to turn right and cross over the dual carriageway. Turn left and proceed ahead. You pass two information panels: one tells of 'Paradise', the other of 'The Blaydon Races'. Now turn right down William Armstrong Drive at the Newcastle Business Park. Cross over an access road and after some 40yds go down the steps on the right to join the riverside path. You will follow this path for the next 2½ miles all the way to the Newcastle Quayside.

You come to 'The Hydraulic Crane', the first of a series of

Miners' Memorial
(*Photograph: Graeme Peacock*)

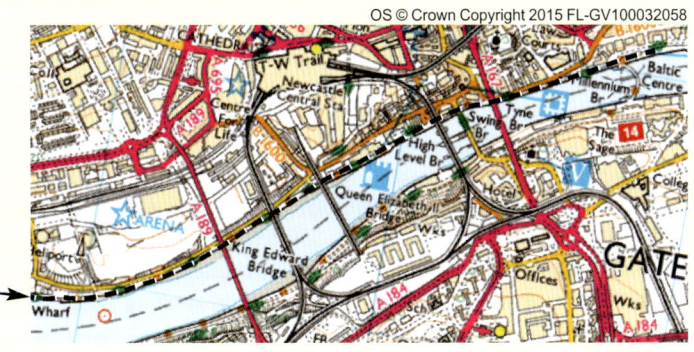

OS © Crown Copyright 2015 FL-GV100032058

Bridges galore (*Photograph: Graeme Peacock*)

information panels detailing Lord Armstrong's engineering works and the industrial heritage of the Scotswood-Elswick area. You pass a number of public art works which may test your imagination and there are benches from which you can admire the developments taking place on the other side of the river. Look out in particular for the wooden loading jetty, the Dunston Staithes, a further reminder of the former importance of the river to the coal trade. The wide expanse of mud flats at low tide in this area enables you to appreciate the tidal nature of the River Tyne.

Subsequently, behind the information panel, 'Armstrong's Works', is a vestige of the machine shop in the form of the arched arcade. You pass a small parade of units including refreshments opportunities. Eventually you come to the end of the Business Park and the bridges gradually come into view – all seven! Proceed ahead under the most recent version of the Redheugh Road Bridge (1983), the King Edward VII Rail Bridge (1906) and the blue Queen Elizabeth II Metro Bridge (1980).

You pass modern hotels, as well as the much older building housing The Quayside pub, before going under the oldest of the current bridges, the High Level Bridge (1849). Notice on the left hand-side abutment, a plaque commemorating 'the father of modern rowing', Harry Clasper. You pass the former Fish Market (1880) with its roof-top sculptures of Neptune and two fishwives. Walk beneath the access road to the Swing Bridge (1876). On the left is the Guildhall, the centre of local government from the 17th century until 1858. It is used on ceremonial occasions, for example, by the Freemen of the city, and it contains some office accommodation.

Finally the Trail leads beneath the Tyne Bridge (1928). Across the river you will recognise Gateshead's emblematic The Glasshouse International Centre for Music (2004) (formerly The Sage), together with the Baltic Centre for Contemporary Art (2002). As you walk along the Newcastle Quayside, you pass the fine facades of some former business premises, the Customs House (1776) and the much more modern Law Courts (1990). Then at last you are at the Gateshead Millennium Bridge and the end of this stage.

Iconic ending

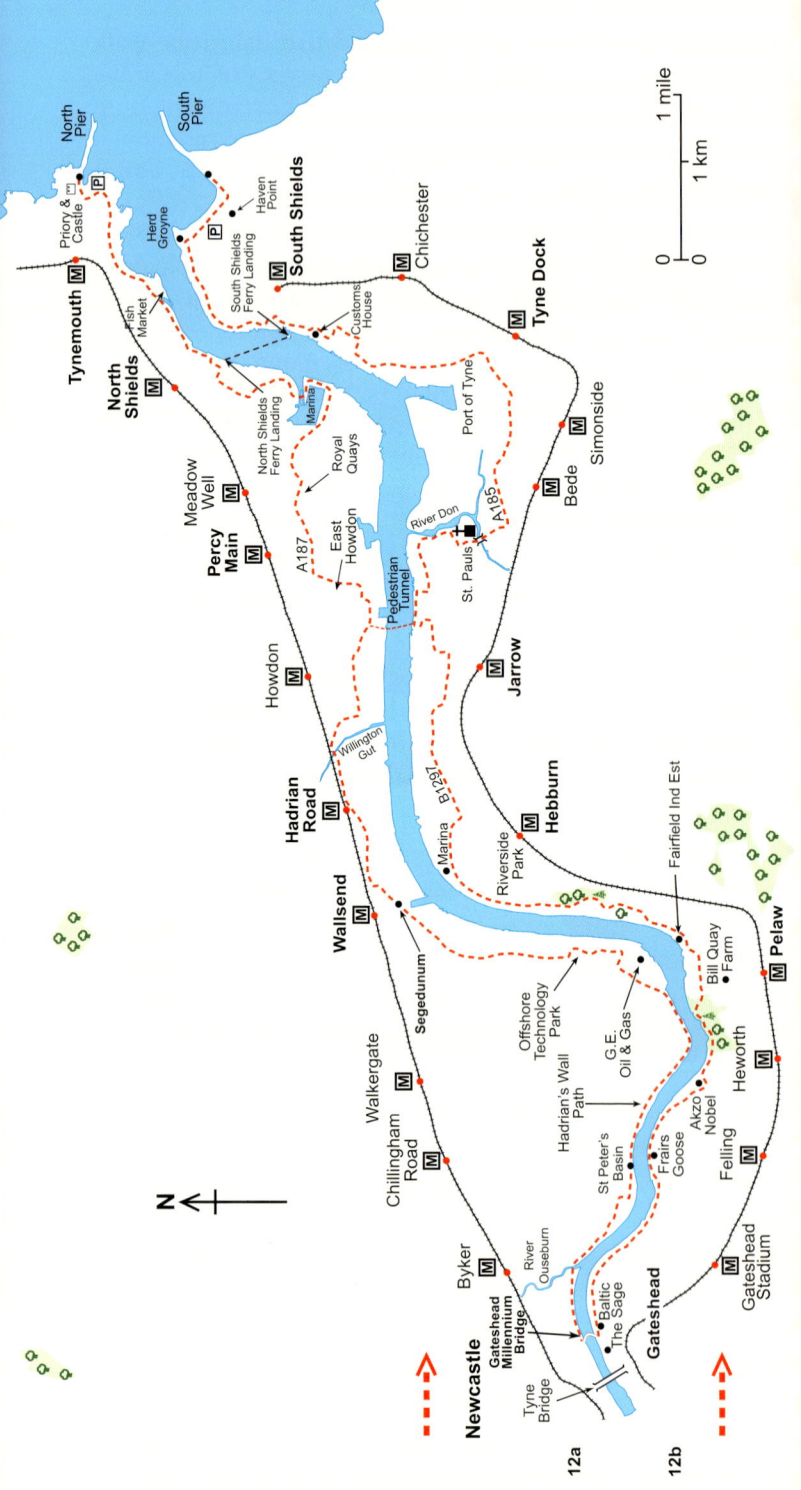

STAGE 12
Newcastle to the sea
13½ miles (21.7km)*

As the sea can be reached by walking down the north or the south side of the River Tyne, or even by crossing from one side to the other through the pedestrian tunnel or by ferry, the distances may vary accordingly. The two basic routes are set separately below as 12(a) North side of the river to Tynemouth and 12(b) South side of the river to South Shields

12(a) North side of the river to Tynemouth
13½ miles (21.7km)

Initially, the riverside path passes modern offices, dwellings and a marina. It eventually leads through the important offshore technology park, which has replaced the former Walker shipyards. It passes Wallsend, the site of the Roman fort of Segedunum, as well as the former world-renowned Swan Hunter shipyard. A further few miles lead to the Royal Quays shopping outlet, a marina and the Port of Tyne International Passenger Terminal. From here, there is a short steady climb before the Trail descends to the North Shields ferry landing. The route continues ahead past the North Shields Fish Quay, along a lengthy promenade and

Entry/exit points	**Newcastle and Gateshead Quaysides GR257640); Metro Stations at Wallsend 5½ miles (8.8km); Hadrian Road 6 miles (9.7km); Percy Main 8¼ miles (13.2km); bus stops at Royal Quays 8¾ miles (14km); North Shields 11 miles (17.7km); Tynemouth 13½ miles (22.1km)**
Maps	**OS Explorer 316 Newcastle upon Tyne; Tyne & Wear A-Z Street Atlas**
Refreshments	**Newcastle and Gateshead Quaysides; Royal Quays; North Shields Fish Quay; Tynemouth village centre**

Brian Burnie leads the way (*Photograph: Tony Iley*)

after a short climb, the Trail descends to the sea and the north pier at Tynemouth.

The walk
You start from the Newcastle side of the Gateshead Millennium Bridge. On your left you pass the Malmaison Hotel, the Pitcher and Piano pub, the sculptures, Swirle Pavilion, the Blacksmith Needle, impressive-looking office blocks and modern apartments. After about ½ mile, you reach the confluence of the Ouseburn and the River Tyne.

Follow the path as it bears left to exit onto a road. Turn sharp right and proceed ahead, crossing a bridge, to arrive at the east side of the River Ouseburn. Continue on the roadside path to arrive at Spiller's Car Park and the Hub cycle shop and café. The riverside path lies invitingly ahead. (At the time of writing its use is permissive, courtesy of Newcastle City Council, and, should the path be closed for any reason, you would need to follow the narrow pavement on the left-hand side of the road.) As you walk along the quayside, you may see a notice advising that there is no exit ahead for pedestrians and cyclists. However, at the end of the paved riverside path, just before reaching a second set of stone bollards, you need to turn left and make your way across the car park to a small gate in the metal fence. Exit through the gate, cross the road with care, turn right and proceed ahead on the narrow pavement to a junction.

Cross the junction with care and continue ahead, bearing

OS © Crown Copyright 2015 FL-GV100032058

left. Follow the road, using the pavement on the right-hand side. You pass between the Bel Valves works and arrive at a crossroads. Turn right and walk down towards the river. After about 100yds, look out for a sign for Hadrian's Way. Turn left and continue along the road (Bottlehouses Street) to enter an area of modern housing (St Peter's Basin). At the junction turn right and walk to the riverside, passing The Merchants Tavern and the Marina. Turn left and continue ahead. Once safely across the access bridge and past the Marina Office, simply follow the pavement as it continues along the riverside.

When you come to the end of the housing you join a surfaced path which you will follow for the next 1¼ miles. Ignore paths and road off, as the Trail keeps close to the riverside. The riverside path leads up a short flight of steps.

Marina Office

OS © Crown Copyright 2015 FL-GV100032058

Eventually, you arrive at a fork in the path, at a brick wall with three inset seating spaces. Bear left on the same surfaced path you have been following, as it leaves the riverside. At the top of the short rise, turn left and then almost immediately right. Follow the path with the perimeter fence on your right as it descends to an access road (Wincomblee Road) at the entrance to GE Oil and Gas. Turn left and proceed ahead on the pavement past various offshore-subsea industry companies.

Roman history

After about ½ mile, turn left, walk about 75yds up the road (Malaya Drive) and turn right in the direction, 'Cycleway 72, Wallsend 1½, Tynemouth 7'. For the next 2 miles or so, the track follows the line of an old railway. At one point, in the absence of the bridge, the path descends to cross a road before climbing back on the other side. You pass some renovated post-World War II prefab housing. The path descends to cross another road before climbing back to continue along the track.

After going under a road bridge, a red sign points right to 'Roman Baths'. It is worth detouring some 25yds to the site of the baths which were re-discovered in 2014. Once back on the track, you pass an interesting location sign as you approach the remains of the Roman fort of Segedunum, at aptly named Wallsend. A metal gate on the left provides access to the museum. Visitors are welcome to use the café and gift shop. On crossing a small bridge, to the right, you will see the entrance to the former shipyard of Swan Hunter (1860-2007). A few yards further, a ramp on the left leads to an access road from where you can walk a further ¼ mile to Wallsend Metro Station should you wish to stop at this point.

A sign on your right indicates 'Hadrian's Cycleway 72; Royal Quays 3½; North Shields 5'. Continue ahead on the surfaced path to cross an access road and further cycleway signs. After about ½ mile you reach a red archway marked 'Hadrian's Cycleway 72' and the end of the surfaced path. Proceed ahead along the shared cycle/pedestrian pavement. Cross Davy Bank and turn left to cross the road to follow the

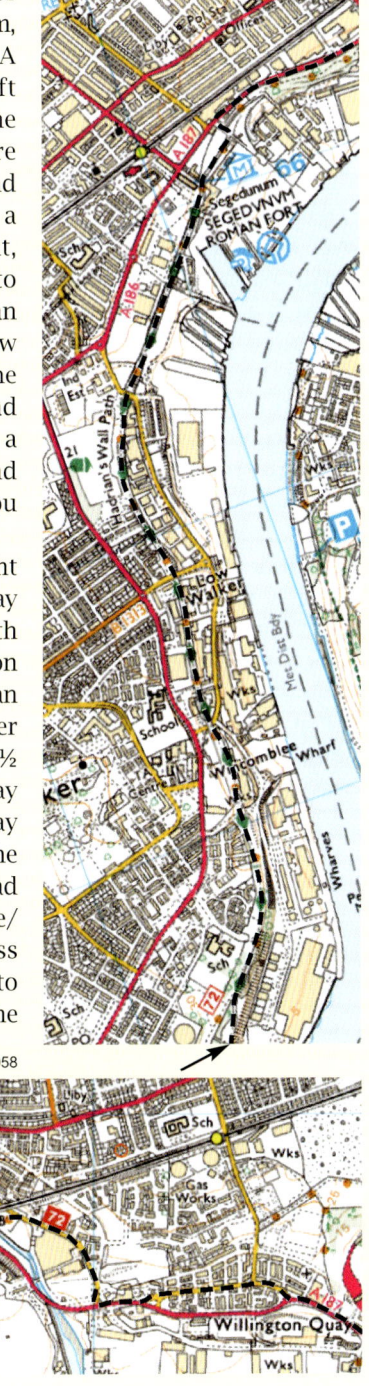

OS © Crown Copyright 2015 FL-GV100032058

cycleway sign 'C2C'. Turn right and continue along the pavement next to the A187 (Hadrian Road) for about ½ mile.

In a short while, you pass an entrance to Hadrian Road Metro Station- another possible escape route for a weary walker! The path descends and at a fork bear left through the trees, hopefully leaving the right-hand path for cyclists! On the left, you should see the imposing Willington Viaduct (1839) now carrying the Metro line. A metal bridge leads over the Willington Gut which flows into the Tyne via the small Willington Quay Marina. The path then crosses through a pleasant grassy area. You join a minor road and bear right to follow the 'Cycleway72 Tynemouth' sign. On the right, you pass Bridon Bekaet rope works.

Continue along the pavement to follow the road as it bears right past the Albion Inn (closed at the time of writing). You return to the main road (Hadrian Road). Turn left, walk straight ahead to pass the Jet Filling Station and the 'Welcome to Willington Quay' sign and proceed along the minor road (Bewicke Road) which eventually bears right towards a roundabout where you rejoin Hadrian Road.

Continue on the left-hand pavement crossing Cumberland Street, where there is a sign to St Paul's Centre and Church. After a few more yards, turn right at the small Tyne Cycle & Ped Tunnel sign and use the traffic lights to cross the main road. Walk ahead and turn left to follow the railings on your right. On the left, you should see the tall office building housing TT2 (the operating and management company of the Tyne Tunnels since 2007) and a Tyne Tunnel ventilation tower. You pass an information panel about North Tyneside Waggonways, just beyond which is the access road that leads to the Tyne Pedestrian and Cycle Tunnels.

OS © Crown Copyright 2015 FL-GV100032058

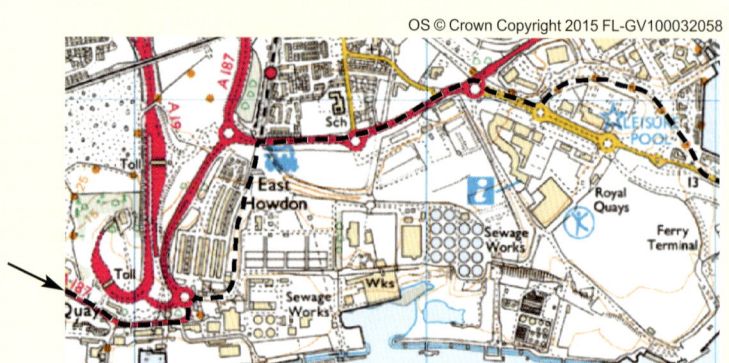

Here you have the opportunity, should you wish, to cross under the river and continue down the south side of the Tyne. See page 139 for details of the walk from the tunnel exit.

Continuing ahead, the path soon bears left past a sign indicating a number of routes ahead. As the path rises, you pass Ristorante Sambuca, formerly a dockland pub, the Duke of Wellington. A few steps ahead, on a grassy slope, is a small metal sculpture *Subway to the south* after which you turn right to walk along Lesbury Street. You pass a children's play area and then turn left into Chatton Street. Proceed, using the ample grass verge, if appropriate, to the end of what is now Baird Avenue. Walk ahead at the sign 'Safer Routes to School' and follow the surfaced path which leads through an underpass brightly adorned with bold graffiti (legal, Phoenix Youth Project, art site).

To continue from the underpass, turn sharp right and follow the ramp up to return again to the main road (A187). Cross over at the pedestrian light and turn left to walk ahead on the shared path for the next ½ mile. You pass a roundabout (the road to the left leads to Percy Main Metro Station in about ¼ mile). Continue ahead and at the next roundabout leave the A187 to take the second road on your right. Walk down Coble Dene. On your right is the Royal Quays Outlet Centre (1966) where you are sure to find a cup of coffee after walking some 8¾ miles!

However, to continue the walk, proceed to the pedestrian lights. Turn left, cross Coble Dene, walk ahead a few yards and turn right onto Hadrian's Cycleway. You may be heartened by the sign indicating the distances, 'Shields Ferry 1½ miles; North Shields Fish Quay 2¼ miles; Tynemouth 3 miles' – although the end of the walk is actually a little further! Follow the path as it gently winds its way down towards the river through Redburn Dene Park, another fine example of the regeneration of much of the riverside.

Ignore paths off and carry on in the same direction until you arrive at a road. Cross the road and proceed ahead in the direction indicated by the 'Cycleways C2C, 10 & 72' signs. Ahead you might see a cruise liner or one of the North Sea ferries which dock at the Port of Tyne International Passenger Terminal. The path leads down to the Royal Quays Marina. The cycleway turns left here but the Trail bears to the right to go around the Marina in an anti-clockwise direction.

You soon get close to the riverside and pass the Earl of Zetland, a permanently moored bar/restaurant and functions facility. A red metal sculpture, *Tyne Anew* stands on the corner as the path turns left. On your right, you pass the former Accumulator Tower, now a listed building, installed in 1882 to operate the lock gates. You soon reach the Royal Quays Marina reception building where you turn right (unless you wish to enjoy refreshments at The Lock café which lies straight ahead).

Reclaimed parkland

Now walk across the first of two permissive walkways over the docks. (Warning lights will alert you to any temporary closures. If the lock is in the process of filling, walk a little further to the second walkway. In the very unlikely event of both walkways being closed for a long time, you would need to retrace your steps to the entrance to the marina and follow the cycleway route!)

Once across the walkways, turn immediately right along the riverside path with some modern housing on your left. The surfaced path soon climbs between the trees away from the riverside. (Further developments should enable you to continue along the waterside all the way to the North Shields

Royal Quays Marina

Ferry landing). Turn right immediately after the metal barrier and continue up a narrow surfaced path parallel to an access road. At the top of the rise, bear right to follow the road as it descends past further housing developments and two modern high-rise buildings. You pass a turning circle for the bus service and a few yards on the right lies the ferry landing.

Proceed ahead with an information panel, part of the North Shields Heritage Trail, on your left. A plaque on the last building indicates that this was originally the Sailors' Home (1856). Walk ahead and cross with care over Borough Road, to a further information panel on the corner.

Proceed ahead, crossing over to the right-hand side of the road when convenient. Fine apartments on both sides of the road have replaced what was once a densely packed area around a former dry dock and engineering works. You will see a replica of the 'Wooden Dolly' outside the

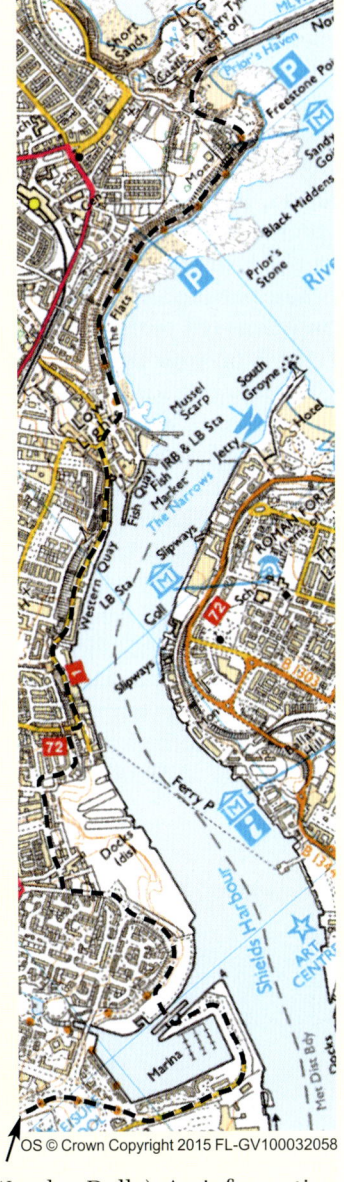

Prince of Wales Tavern (Old Wooden Dolly). An information panel provides an explanation. As you continue ahead, you will see a white tower on the left, the High Light, a former navigational aid. Shortly afterwards, its counterpart, the Low Light, appears ahead as you reach a tall, blue-grey corrugated building, the former ice factory now an events venue.

In a few paces you arrive at North Shields Fish Quay where there is a further information panel. Now follow the quay. On your left, you will find a miscellany of premises, restaurants and cafés where fish is obviously the dish of the day! Notice the decorations and dedications on the walls on the right. Just before the road bears left, with Vita House ahead, turn right to cross the road to a paved area. Walk about 20yds and turn right again. On your left, you pass the Dock Masters House and the Fishermen's Mission with its ornate balcony. At the end of the Mission building, turn left onto a paved path. As you proceed ahead the white Low Light is on your right and as you bear left, the remains of Clifford's Fort (the relevant information panel lies a few hundred yards ahead). Follow the wall of the fort and after a sharp left-hand bend, cross the road to walk up the ramp to rejoin the riverside path. You then pass the impressive sculpture, *Fiddlers Green*, dedicated to the memory of fishermen lost at sea.

Now, at last, the mouth of the Tyne comes fully into view, although you still have some way to walk! Proceed ahead to pass three colourfully-restored navigation buoys and the Clifford's Fort information panel on your left, as well as a small beach on your right. Ahead are splendid views of the north and south piers. On the opposite side of the river, you will see a riverside wall, Herd Groyne, with its red

Castle and Priory

lighthouse built in 1882 before the piers were constructed. It still acts as a navigational aid.

As you proceed along the promenade, towering above the bankside are the 1930s Sir James Knott Memorial Flats. Inevitably the eye is drawn to the tall and imposing monument dedicated to Admiral Lord Collingwood (1748-1810). You will find details on the relevant information panel as you proceed ahead. You soon reach a further information panel, 'Shipwrecks and Heroes', and the notorious Black Midden rocks are recalled on a small plaque on the railings a short distance ahead.

Eventually, the path ascends quite steeply, passing a sign indicating the end of the C2C cycle route. At the top of the rise, you join an access road and on your left is Tynemouth's Volunteer Life Brigade's Watch House and Museum. Ahead, on the cliff top, stand Tynemouth Priory and Castle (English Heritage). Below, on the right, are Tynemouth Rowing Club and Tynemouth Sailing Club.

Follow the road down and go over the small bridge. Tynemouth village lies ahead up the steep bank with its Metro Station about ½ mile away. However, to complete the walk you need to turn right here at the 'Welcome to North Pier' sign. Continue down the path where, a short distance before the pier, a very welcoming marker stone on the left announces that you have reached the end of the River Tyne Trail. Well done and hearty congratulations! Just make sure you have your photo taken beside the stone!

Tynemouth

Tynemouth (population approx 68,000), with its fine beaches, aquarium, castle and priory is a popular place to live as well as for day visits. Conveniently, it lies within easy commuting distance of Newcastle and Gateshead. The Victorian railway station, now a stop on the Tyne and Wear Metro, hosts a comprehensive arts and crafts market every Saturday and Sunday. Tynemouth Village, centred round Front Street, boasts an eclectic collection of shops as well as many pubs, cafés and restaurants.

12(b) South side of the river to South Shields
13½ miles (21.7km)

From the south end of the Gateshead Millennium Bridge you pass the Baltic Centre for Contemporary Art. After a short industrial section the Trail joins a pleasant riverside path. It leads past a small marina before detouring around an important industrial site. It then passes through a riverside park, an impressive example of the reclamation work. The Trail goes past an important 7th-century monastic site before passing the modern Port of Tyne facilities. Finally you walk along a pleasantly renovated promenade as the River Tyne reaches the sea and you reach South Shields pier.

Entry/exit points	Newcastle and Gateshead Quaysides (GR257640); Metro stations at Pelaw 3¾ miles (6km); Hebburn 5¼ miles (8.2km); Jarrow 7½ miles (12km); Tyne Dock 10 miles (16km); South Shields (ferry landing) 11¾ miles (18.9km); South Shields (pier) 13½ miles (21.7km)
Maps	OS Explorer 316 Newcastle upon Tyne; Tyne & Wear A-Z Street Atlas
Refreshments	Newcastle and Gateshead Quaysides; Friars Goose Marina; The Customs House, South Shields; Haven Point, cafés & restaurants in South Shields centre

The Walk
From the Newcastle end of the Gateshead Millennium Bridge cross over into Baltic Square, turn left and walk ahead to the left of the Baltic Centre for Contemporary Art. Turn right at the bollards before Jury's Inn and then left to join the road (South Shore Road). Continue straight ahead passing a miscellaneous collection of workshops and business premises that unfortunately impede views of the river. However, after about ½ mile you catch a brief glimpse of the Tyne just before you turn right at Tarmac works entrance. Walk uphill for about 50yds and turn left at a

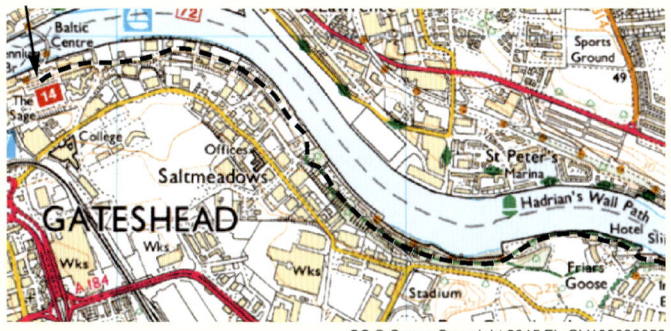

OS © Crown Copyright 2015 FL-GV100032058

cycleway sign. You pass a further number of industrial sites before the road eventually descends to the riverside with a pleasant sweep of the Tyne ahead.

Turn left at the next set of bollards and go down a flight of steps. (Alternatively you can keep straight ahead on a higher path for about 300yds until the paths converge near a car park.) You walk through a car park and immediately bear left.

Proceed to a junction,

Crossing to The Baltic
(*Photograph: Graeme Peacock*)

where you turn left downhill to continue along the pleasant riverside path. The path affords good views across the river and after a while you will be able to identify the modern housing and marina at St Peter's Basin. You reach some apartments as the road climbs steeply between them and the Rivers Hotel. On the left, beyond the hotel, is the small Friars Goose Marina and café, while on the right you will find an anchor resting on a stone. A plaque explains that this area, like many you will encounter on your journey down the Tyne, has been reclaimed from former heavy industrial usages.

After about 75yds, as the road bears right, turn left and then go immediately right to follow the cycleway. The surfaced path climbs slowly between the trees. Care needs to be taken to look out for cyclists. The path leads to a more

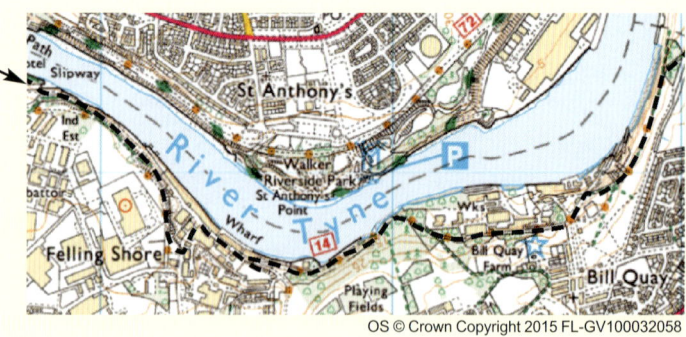

open space. Eventually, below, you see the rooftops of the Akzo Nobel industrial plant. You lose sight of the river for a while as the path diverts around the plant and joins an access road. Turn left and follow the road as it turns right at the entrance to the site.

Follow the road as it climbs steadily for 400yds, then turn left at a cycleway sign into Abbotsford Road where there are light industrial premises. Continue for about 125yds and make sure not to miss the narrow path on the left, just before KGM Refrigeration and opposite Tuffnells Parcels Express loading bays. Pass between the metal barriers and go down the path with the Akzo Nobel complex on your left and then housing on your right. You arrive at an access road with corrugated fencing on your right, behind which are stables. Cross the road and go between the bollards to

Friars Goose Marina

rejoin the cycleway at the riverside.

Continue ahead along the undulating path. After a while you lose sight of the river and you find a high wall on the left. You reach an access road to the Fairfield Industrial Park. This was once part of the thriving dock area of Bill Quay. Cross the road to continue ahead on the Keelman's Way and cycle route. To your right is The Cricketers pub. The path bears left, beside a grassy area, and then right, as it climbs between the trees.

At a junction, bear left to enter South Tyneside. The river comes back into view. The path reaches a junction after a bollard. Turn left and

descend to the riverside to meet an access road which you follow to the right. Hebburn Riverside Park on your right provides yet another example of reclamation from the heavy industrial sites that once dominated this area.

You arrive at a boardwalk-jetty with convenient benches and a car park. At the end of the boardwalk an information panel tells of local industrial and social heritage.

Follow the road for about 250yds, passing Hebburn Marina and Boat Club, before turning left at the NCR 14 sign

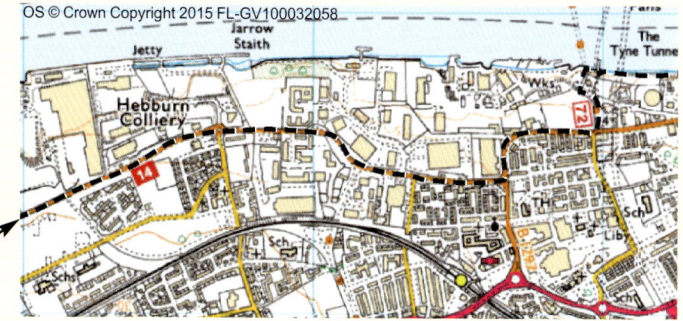

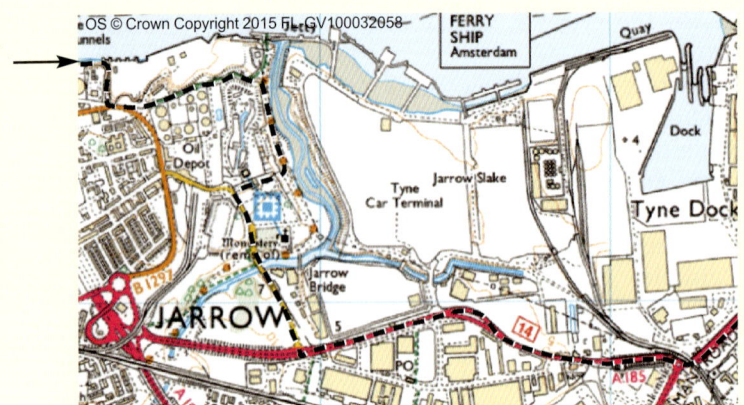

'South Shields-Pedestrian Tunnel – Jarrow'. (If required, Hebburn Metro Station is about ¼ mile further up the road – Prince Consort Road.) Continue along the path (Hebburn Cycleway) for a few hundred yards passing the TS Kelly Sea Cadets' premises. Bear left to descend once more to a riverside path and some pleasant modern housing. Follow the road as it climbs past the boarded-up former Hawthorn Leslie shipyard. Standing out ahead is the exceedingly tall spire of St Andrew's Presbyterian/URC Church (see information panel).

A short distance further up the road you arrive at the T-junction (Lyon Street) where you turn left. The river now

Hebburn boardwalk

remains out of sight and you need to be prepared for about 2 miles of roadside walking until you reach the Pedestrian Tunnel. Follow the busy straight road (B1297), the name of which changes after the first roundabout from Lyon Street to Waggonway Road. Happily, in contrast to signs of dereliction, you will see some activity as you pass the entrance to A&P ship repairs, conversion, marine and energy services.

When you reach Windmill Way roundabout, ahead you should be able to see the tall ventilation shaft of the Tyne Tunnel. Carry straight on as the road becomes Blackett Street and then Western Road. Eventually, you arrive at a roundabout near the centre of Jarrow. If you wish to seek refreshments or you feel you have come far enough after walking about 7 miles, turn right for local amenities and Jarrow Metro Station.

However, to continue on the Trail, turn left and follow the road (B1297) for about a mile. On the right you will see a Tyne Tunnel ventilation tower while the Tyne Pedestrian and Cycle Tunnels entrances lie to the left. You might like to walk down and visit the entrance and enjoy the view of the river from the riverside park. (Here you have the opportunity, should you wish, to walk beneath the river and continue the Trail down the north side of the Tyne. See page 129 for details of the walk from the tunnel exit on the north side of the river.)

To continue down the south side of the river, continue ahead on the B1297 for about ¼ mile before turning left just

Tyne Pedestrian Tunnel

before a gasometer and the exit to Cemex Jarrow Wharf. Bear right and walk past the bollards to follow the surfaced path as it descends to an access road near the River Don. At the junction, bear slightly left to join the clear, but narrow, riverside path (otherwise, if the path looks very muddy you can continue along the access road). The path rejoins the road and you pass a car park area.

Follow the road as it turns right at some boulders. After about 100yds, on the left, you arrive at an entrance gate into the grounds of St Paul's Church and Monastery. This is an important site associated with the noted 7th-century monk and historian, The Venerable Bede. (Time permitting, you then have a number of options. Go through the gateway to visit the church and/or the site. While opposite, on the right-hand side of the road, a path leads through the parkland to the 18th-century Jarrow Hall which contains a pleasant café.)

To proceed on the Trail, continue ahead along the access road and turn left at the main road (Church Bank). Proceed ahead. At the beginning of the bridge, there is an information panel about the old Jarrow

OS © Crown Copyright 2015 FL-GV100032058

Church and Monastery

Bridge, said to be part of a medieval route to the monastery. There is no pavement on this side of the road, however, you can take advantage of the generous grass verge or use the pavement on the other side of the road. At the bottom of the road turn left and walk along the shared pedestrian/cycle path parallel to the road. Be prepared for the fact that the next 1.75 miles or so lead alongside the A185 and A194, through the busy industrial area of Tyne Dock, dominated by the Port of Tyne facilities which include the cruise and North Sea ferry terminals.

Proceed ahead past the Port of Tyne Jarrow Slake entrance with its important car terminal. After going beneath a bridge, there is a further panel with the rather grim title, 'Slime-dripping Arches'. Here you will find information about the prolific writer Catherine Cookson as well as about Tyne Dock.

You arrive at a further entrance to the Port of Tyne at Tyne Dock. Cross the access road with care to pass Navigation House. A sign indicates that Tyne Dock Metro Station is ¼ mile to the right. At the roundabout turn left in the direction 'Riverside B1302'. Look out for a bench behind which are three metal figures of local significance (Sarah Milligan, comedian; a Roman centurion and Norman Fry, cycle maker). Ignore the sign indicating 'New Route' to the right and instead keep to the left, with Kennedy's pub on the right. The busy road passes the Port of Tyne Warehouse Service as it climbs for about ¾ mile. At the top of the rise as the road bears right you need to turn left down an access road.

Chance to cross

Walk down the access road (West Holburn). Through the railings, you will see the Port of Tyne International Terminal and possibly one of the DFDS Seaways vessels. Follow the road which turns right to join Commercial Road. Turn left to pass the Trimmers Arms and then, on the right, South Tyneside Law Courts. Watch out after about 100yds, to turn left to leave the roadside path. Walk down the narrow path and descend thirteen steps towards a housing complex (to avoid the steps you could continue straight ahead). Keep to the left, ignoring the first road on your right, and follow the road as it bears right, then left with the tall Mill Dam (1865) on the right. The name comes from the 13th-century mill that once stood here. In a few paces you arrive at The Customs House, the former Board of Trade Shipping Office (1863), restored and extended in 1994 as an entertainment and arts centre. The Green Room bar-bistro-coffee shop is open every day.

Make your way to the riverside where there are excellent views. Facing the river, next to The Customs House and now private accommodation, is the former River Police and Tyne Port Sanitary Authority building of 1886. A plaque provides details. From The Customs House walk ahead, past the poignant Merchant Navy memorial. Continue along the neatly redeveloped riverside path and in a short distance you reach the South Shields ferry landing. South Shields pier and the end of the walk lies about 2½ miles ahead. Here you have your last opportunity to cross the river should you wish to end the walk at Tynemouth.

To continue from the South Shields ferry landing, with the river on your left, walk along the riverside promenade now regenerated with modern dwellings. You simply need to keep close to the riverside. You cross the walkway over a former dry dock and pass a flagpole with compass points marked in the stone surrounds. Just before a larger former

OS © Crown Copyright 2015 FL-GV100032058

dock, you'll find the welcome sight of a small damsel clutching a ship and waving a greeting in the form of Irene Brown's sculpture *Spirit of South Shields*.

The path joins the road where you turn left. However, it is worth crossing to the other side of the road for a moment to an extension of the dock where there is *Fleet*, a further art work by Irene Brown. Continue alongside the road passing South Quays apartments, South Shields Sea Cadets premises and Comical Corner, the strange name apparently reflecting rather awkward nearby river currents. You are now on Wapping Street with its fascinating variety of businesses, boatyards, slipways and also a Marine School.

Wapping Street joins a main road (River Drive) at the bottom of a hill. You need to cross over the road, with care, to use the pavement on the other side. Walk along the right-hand pavement, and then cross back to the other side of the road again when the pavement resumes on the left. Soon there is further evidence of regeneration as modern housing comes into view. Turn left at the access road into the attractive properties of Harbour View. Follow the road as it bears left and then right to arrive via a few steps to a further riverside promenade. Turn right and walk along the promenade where you can enjoy the good views across to the North Shields Fish Quay, the 1930s James Knott Memorial Flats towering above on the bankside, the Priory and Castle at Tynemouth and the tall and imposing monument dedicated to the memory of Admiral Lord Collingwood, hero of the naval Battle of Trafalgar (1805).

River Tyne joins the sea

Follow the path which turns inland and, at the end of the railings, go down the steps and walk the short distance across the tiny bay to reach a riverside path where you turn left. Proceed along the path as it hugs the riverside with The Little Haven Hotel on the right. At a junction, you reach a panel with historical details of the North and South piers and the Herd Groyne. A few yards ahead, along the groyne or riverside wall, is the Port of Tyne's Herd Groyne Lighthouse.

However, to continue on the Trail you need to turn right at the information panel and follow the path, with the hotel on your right. You walk through the artwork *Conversation Piece* by the Spanish sculptor Juan Munoz (1999). Bear left to climb a short set of steps that lead to the result of another regeneration project: Littlehaven promenade, seawall and coastal park.

Follow the promenade around the bay. On the upper walkway is the sculpture *Eye* (Stephen Broadbent, 2014), while along the promenade you pass a series of 'portholes' before arriving at *Sail*, a further work by the same artist. The tall modern building to the right is Haven Point (2013) leisure facility which includes a visitor centre and café.

You now need to walk along the pier for about 350yds, just past Watch House, the headquarters of South Shields Volunteer Life Brigade (founded 1866), to reach the marker stone indicating the official end of the River Tyne Trail. Congratulations, well done and make sure to take a photo or two!

(To return to Newcastle, you need to retrace your steps back along the pier, cross over the road and make your way up Ocean Road towards the centre of South Shields with its amenities including the Metro Station about a mile away, or to North Shields via the ferry, a further ¼ mile away).

South Shields

With a population of over 80,000 South Shields is the second largest town in the Tyneside conurbation. Following the demise of traditional shipbuilding and mining, service industries and tourism now provide important inputs into the local economy.

In addition to its six miles of beaches and two attractive parks, the town centre offers a wide range of amenities, including: its museum and art gallery, a fascinating collection of ethnic restaurants and a noted fish and chips venue.

RIVER TYNE TRAIL
SEA TO SOURCES

	miles	(kms)	page
Section 1: River Tyne			
Stage 1 The sea to Newcastle	13½	(21.7)	147
Stage 2 Newcastle to Wylam	10¾	(17.3)	155
Stage 3 Wylam to Corbridge	13¼	(21.3)	158
Stage 4 Corbridge to Warden	7½	(12.1)	162
	45	**(72.4)**	
Section 2: River North Tyne			
Stage 5 Warden to Barrasford	7	(11.3)	165
Stage 6 Barrasford to Bellingham	13¼	(21.3)	168
Stage 7 Bellingham to Kielder Dam	12¼	(19.7)	172
Stage 8 Kielder Dam to Source of North Tyne	15½	(25.0)	176
	48	**(77.3)**	
Section 3: River South Tyne			
Stage 9 Warden to Haydon Bridge	6½	(10.5)	179
Stage 10 Haydon Bridge to Haltwhistle	12	(19.3)	181
Stage 11 Haltwhistle to Alston	13¾	(22.1)	186
Stage 12 Alston to Source of South Tyne	9¾	(15.7	190
	42	**(67.6)**	
	135	**(217.3)**	

STAGE 1
The sea to Newcastle
13½ miles (21.7km)

As Newcastle can be reached by walking down the north or the south side of the River Tyne, or even by crossing from one side to the other through the pedestrian tunnel or by ferry, the distances may vary accordingly. The two basic routes are set separately below as 1(a) Tynemouth to Newcastle and 1(b) South Shields to Newcastle.

1(a) Tynemouth to Newcastle

Entry/exit points	Tynemouth; North Shields 2 miles (3.2km); Percy Main 4¾ miles (7.7km); Hadrian Road 7 miles (11.2km); Metro Station at Wallsend 7½ miles (12.1km); Newcastle and Gateshead Quaysides 13 miles (20.9km)
Map	See Sketch Map on Page 122 OS Explorer 316 Newcastle upon Tyne; Tyne & Wear A-Z Street Atlas
Refreshments	Tynemouth village centre; North Shields Fish Quay; Royal Quays; Newcastle and Gateshead Quaysides

The Trail starts at the Daft as a Brush marker stone near the beginning of Tynemouth pier. Return to the access road and turn left. Follow the road as it passes the Volunteer Life Brigade's Watch House on the right, before descending to the River Tyne. Follow the promenade for about ¾ mile. The path bears left and passes *Fiddlers Green*, the

Marker stone at Tynemouth

fishermen's memorial. Continue ahead to follow the path with the walls of the 17th-century Cliffords Fort on your right. A narrow passage leads past the tall, white Low Light building into an open space with the Fishermen's Mission on your right. Continue ahead a short way before turning left to join a road through North Shields Fish Quay. Now follow the road, ignoring roads off, to pass the entrance to North Shields Ferry Landing. (There are plans to re-locate this adjacent to the Fish Quay.)

North Shields Fish Quay

The road bears right as it climbs through modern developments. At the top of the rise bear left to join a cycle way/pedestrian path parallel to an access road (Ballast Hill Road). After about 125yds, turn left through a gap in the metal barrier and follow the surfaced path to the riverside. Turn right and continue to the end of the path. Turn left, cross over the permissive walkway and proceed around three sides of Royal Quays Marina to an access road through the reclaimed parkland (Redburn Dene Park).

Turn left at the waymark, 'Tyne Cycle & Pedestrian Tunnel 1.25miles; Segedunum 3 mile; Newcastle Quayside 8 miles', and use the pedestrian lights to cross the road (Coble Dene). Turn right, follow the road, with Royal Quays Outlet Centre on your left up to a roundabout. Take the second road on your left to join the A187. Continue past a further roundabout. After 170yds cross over the dual carriageway using the pedestrian lights and head down a ramp which bears left leading you to an underpass. Once through the underpass, the path becomes Baird Avenue and then Chatton Street. At the end of the row of houses turn right into Lesbury Street. Turn left at the junction and follow the road as it descends past the Sambuca restaurant. Continue ahead and bear right past the access road to the Tyne Pedestrian and Cycle Tunnels. Eventually the path bears right to the main road (Hadrian Road) which you cross via the traffic lights. Turn left and as the main road bears left, continue straight ahead on the minor road (Bewicke Road). You pass a Jet filling station before you turn right at the next junction. This minor road passes Bridon Bekaet rope works. Turn left through a grassy area and walk over the metal bridge. The surfaced path then rises quite steeply to meet the main road (Hadrian Road).

Turn right and follow the shared roadside path for about ½ mile until you come to a junction. Turn left to follow the 'Cycleway 72' sign as it crosses Davy Bank and then turn right along the shared pavement. Eventually you pass under a red archway and follow the path as it makes its way past the remains of the Roman fort Segedunum on the right and the former site of Swan Hunter's shipyard on your left. Continue along the path as it follows the old waggonway. The path crosses over Welbeck Road and then continues for about ½ mile before you turn left at the next road (Malaya Drive) in the direction 'Cycleway 72'.

Turn right at the T-junction onto an access road, Wincomblee Road. At the end of the road, turn right and follow the path as it climbs away from the industrial estate. At a junction, at the top of the rise turn left, then almost immediately right. The path leads down to the riverside. Continue along the path for about 1¼ miles to St Peters Basin where you cross a walkway at the Marina. Keep to the riverside and at the end of the apartment block (Chandlers Quay) turn right and proceed ahead to take the first road on the left, Bottlehouses Street. This road eventually leads to a large engineering works (Bel Valves), turn right to walk away from the river to a crossroads.

Turn left and follow the road as it descends to what was once Spillers Quay, now subject to redevelopment as a leisure attraction. Bear right and follow the road to the Hub Cycle shop and café. Continue ahead crossing a bridge over the tributary River Ouseburn. After about 200yds, turn left and make your way to rejoin the riverside path. Continue along this path until you arrive at the Gateshead Millennium Bridge and the end of this stage of the Trail.

St Peter's Basin

Welcome sight

Stage 1b South Shields to Newcastle

Entry/exit points	South Shields; Tyne Dock 4 miles (6.5km); Jarrow 6½ miles (10.5km); Hebburn 8 ¾ miles (14.3km); Metro Station at Pelaw 10 ¼ miles (16.5km); Newcastle and Gateshead Quaysides 14 miles (22.5km)
Map	See Sketch Map on Page 122 OS Explorer 316 Newcastle upon Tyne; Tyne & Wear A-Z Street Atlas
Refreshments	Cafés and restaurants in South Shields centre, Haven Point, Littlehaven Hotel, The Customs House, Friars Goose Marina; Newcastle and Gateshead Quaysides

Start from the Daft as a Brush marker stone about 250yds along the pier just beyond the pier wall. Walk back down the pier, turn right and proceed to the end of the promenade. Continue straight ahead passing the sculptured figures and The Little Haven Hotel until you reach the riverside. Turn left, proceed a short way along the surfaced path and then turn right to cross a small bay. Climb a short

Marker stone at South Shields

flight of steps, turn right and continue along the promenade. Just before the end of the walkway, climb the thirteen steps and proceed through the estate to exit onto the main road (River Drive).

Turn right, follow the road and as it begins to rise, bear right onto Wapping Street in the direction 'Cycleway 72; Pedestrian Ferry'. You pass some boatyards, South Marine College and South Quays apartments. When you reach a dock extension on the left, turn right onto the England Coast Path. Continue along the riverside path to pass the

Ferry Landing before arriving at the Customs House, now an entertainment and arts centre.

From the Customs House, walk inland past the Mill Dam on your left, and bear right to climb gently up the access road to a set of steps after which you join Commercial Road. Turn right and continue as far as the Trimmers Arms where you turn right down a minor road which takes you back to the riverside for a short time before you bear right once more onto Commercial Road. Now follow the busy road for about ¾ mile until you arrive at a major junction.

Here you bear right to continue along the busy roadside though the Tyne Dock area to another important junction where you bear right on the A185 to continue along Cycleway 14. After a further mile you leave the main road to take the first road on your right (Church Bank). Proceed alongside the road (grass verge on right or pavement on left). You cross a bridge over the River Don and after about 200yds, turn right to walk down an access road. St Paul's Church and Monastery are on the right and Jarrow Hall with its café are on the left.

To continue, follow the access road to a junction and turn left. Continue along the road or pick up a path nearer the River Don. After about 750yds, bear left away from the river and follow the surfaced path that climbs to meet a main road (B1297) at Cemex Jarrow Wharf. Turn right and follow the road for about ¼ mile. On the left you pass a Tyne

St Paul's Church and monastery

Tunnel ventilation tower and on the right an access road leads to the Pedestrian and Cycle Tunnels.

Proceed ahead on the B1297 for about a mile and at a roundabout turn right. Continue ahead on the B1297 which in turn bears several names. After about 1½ miles, as a tall spire of the former St Andrew's Church comes clearly into view, turn right down Ellison Street to reach the riverside where you turn left to follow the riverside path. The path climbs away from the river and passes the TS Kelly Sea Cadets centre. Bear right to continue on the cycleway (Hebburn Cycleway) which eventually meets an access road. Turn right and follow the road as it winds back to the riverside. Proceed along the boardwalk/road before turning left to walk up a surfaced path to a junction where you turn right. Continue straight ahead. The path becomes tree-lined before it descends to a junction with The Cricketers pub up on the left.

Landmark spire

Walk straight ahead on the Keelmans Way. After about a mile you cross an access road with corrugated fencing on your left. Follow the path which rises between housing on the left and an industrial complex on the right. The path leads to a road (Abbotsford Road) where you turn right and walk a short distance to a junction. Turn right and follow the road past the entrance to Akzo Nobel. The road bears left and immediately after some business premises you need to turn right onto a narrow surfaced path.

The path descends to meet an access road. Turn right and follow the road as it arrives at Friars Goose with its hotel, café, marina and apartment block where again you join a riverside path. Now continue ahead for about 1½ miles and follow the river until eventually the path climbs steeply to join a road (South Shore Road) which leads through an industrial estate and descends back towards the river to pass a number of workshops and Tarmac. The Baltic arts centre comes into view and you turn right past the car park to reach the riverside and to proceed a short way to Gateshead Millennium Bridge. Cross the bridge over to the Newcastle Quayside to finish this stage of the Trail.

Millennium Bridge

STAGE 2
Newcastle to Wylam
10¾ miles (22.1km)

Entry/exit points	Newcastle and Gateshead Quaysides; Newburn 7½ miles (12.1km); Wylam 10¾ miles (17.3km)
Map	See Sketch Map on Page 112 OS Explorer 316 Newcastle upon Tyne
Refreshments	Pubs and cafés on Newcastle and Gateshead Quaysides; cafés in Newburn Riverside and Newburn Industrial Estate; riverside café and pubs at Newburn; pubs and tearoom in Wylam

From the Newcastle end of the Gateshead Millennium Bridge follow the Tyne upstream under the six other bridges. Eventually you walk past the Newcastle Business Park. The path bears left and leaves the riverside up William Armstrong Drive (named after Lord Armstrong, founder of the Elswick engineering works which once dominated this riverside area) to meet the main A695 (Scotswood Road). Turn left and proceed about 600yds to use the second set of pedestrian lights, at a Hadrian's Way sign, to cross the busy dual carriageway. Turn left, walk about 200yds and then bear right to leave the roadside and continue along the Hadrian's Wall path. Proceed for about ¾ mile, ignoring paths off until you descend to meet Scotswood Road again. Bear right towards a roundabout and use the pedestrian lights to cross over to the left-hand side of the busy dual carriageway.

Resting near Newburn

Turn right and continue alongside the riverside for about 450yds. Bear right to rejoin the roadside path then bear left to cross Lemington Bridge with its ornate white lampposts. After about 400yds turn left at the sign for Newburn Riverside.

Follow the riverside path and after about 2 miles you reach a junction of paths. Turn left onto an access road (Shelley Road) and follow the road through the Newburn Industrial Estate. After about ½ mile, turn right to leave the road, (sign, 'Newburn ½; Wylam 3½') and go up a short track which soon rises to meet a broader path. Bear left and continue along Cycleway 72. Bear left at a fork to reach a road with Newburn Bridge on your left. Great care needs to be taken as you cross over to the other side of the road to join an access road. This takes you past The Boathouse Branzino Restaurant and the clubhouse of Tyne Amateur Rowing Club.

Continue ahead on the access road which joins a surfaced path and winds its way to cross a small bridge to enter the Tyne Riverside Country Park. You pass a car park and a monument to the Battle of Newburn Ford 1640. Follow the riverside path with Hedley's Riverside Café Shop to the right and a slipway on the left. The surfaced path passes a children's play area and picnic benches. After about ¾ miles you arrive at a junction of paths 'Wylam 2 miles'; Here you have a choice of routes:

Tide Stone

Option A (along the riverside for the more sure-footed)

Continue straight ahead and go through a kissing gate to join the riverside path This is narrow and uneven in places and may be slippery in wet weather. After about ½ mile, look out for the Tide Stone close to the fence on your right. The path goes along the edge of a cultivated field and then winds through a tree-lined area. At times the green path gets close to the alternative surfaced path. Eventually the path leads through a more open area and to a kissing gate. Once through the gate turn right. In a short distance you go through another gate and join the broad former waggonway opposite George Stephenson's cottage. Turn left to join the alternative route at A&B below.

Option B (along a former waggonway)

Turn right to follow the public bridleway and NCN72. You pass a row of houses after which you turn left to join an old waggonway, now a broad surfaced path. After about 1¾ miles you reach George Stephenson's Cottage.

Riverside gate

A&B

From Stephenson's Cottage both options now proceed ahead along the waggonway for about ½ mile to the car park at Wylam and the end of this stage of the Trail.

Stephenson's Cottage

STAGE 3
Wylam to Corbridge
13¼ miles (21.2km)

Entry/exit points	Wylam; Prudhoe 4¼ miles (6.8km); Stocksfield 7¼ miles (11.6km); Riding Mill 10¼ miles (16.5km); Corbridge 1¼ miles (21.3km)
Map	See Sketch Map on Page 100 OS Explorer 316 Newcastle upon Tyne; OS Explorer OL43 Hadrian's Wall
Refreshments	Pubs and tearoom in Wylam; riverside café at Prudhoe; hotel in Riding Mill; cafés and pubs in Corbridge

Walk out of the entrance to Wylam Car Park and bear left past the War Memorial and the bridge on your right to join an access road. Once on the access road, turn right and follow the path as it leads under the bridge. The riverside path leads up some steps and passes a terrace of houses and then a sports field on your right. At the end of the cricket

Wylam Bridge

field turn right and follow the path away from the river. At a junction, after about 100yds, turn left and follow the path as it bears left past some allotments and heads down towards the riverside once again. Following the riverside path you will arrive at Hagg Bank Bridge where you cross the River Tyne. Once on the other side, turn immediately right and follow the narrow path which soon leads on to a surfaced undulating riverside track. The track, well used by cyclists, goes through a paddock area and passes some fine properties. If you wish to walk closer to the river, turn right at a small sign, 'No horses, no cycles'. Cross a footbridge and follow one of the well-trodden riverside paths. Rejoin the surfaced track just before the road bridge, and continue ahead. After about 2 miles, on your left beyond the bridge at Prudhoe, you will see the Tyne Countryside Park car park and café.

Crossing Hagg Bank Bridge

Continue ahead for about 300yds before bearing left to arrive at a pedestrian crossing over the railway line. Taking great care to cross the busy line and follow the path as it ascends steeply. As you reach the top of the climb you will see the metal railings of an industrial park on your right. At the end of the railings, bear right on to an access road then almost immediately left onto a signposted byway. Having passed a modern property the path descends steeply between the trees. At a junction, turn right and walk down to cross the railway line with great care. You enter a riverside path through a fishing area. Follow the path as it leads across a small footbridge, up some steps and through a metal gate. Turn left and follow the faint path around two sides of the field edge. The path leads through a tunnel under the railway. Walk up towards the farm buildings with a quarry on the left. Once past the farm, follow the lane until it reaches the A695 and turn right to pass Stocksfield Sports Fields. Follow the pavement alongside this busy road through Stocksfield. Continue ahead. The road bears left at a junction with the road to Bywell on your right. Then, after a few hundred yards, you have a choice of routes:

Option A (the scenic but longer route)
With care, cross over the road to join the minor B6309 Ebchester and Hindley road. After crossing the railway bridge, turn right and walk through the small car park. Leave via the bottom left-hand corner and walk straight ahead. Bear left at a fork in the path to climb between the trees. At a further fork bear right and continue ahead, ignoring paths off. At a junction, follow the fingerpost indicating straight on for Broomley. The broad path leads to a waymarked post where you turn right. Now follow the narrower path where you need to turn left at a corner with a stream ahead. Continue with a fence on your left to leave the woods through a gate. Cross a small plank bridge over the burn before climbing to a field. Continue ahead on the faint path passing a pond on the left. At the right-hand corner of the field go through a gate and turn right to reach a road junction. Walk ahead through Broomley.

After about 500yds, go over a ladder stile on the right at a fingerpost, 'Public Footpath'. Follow the field edge with a fence on your right. Go over a stile, cross a minor road and go through a gap in the hedge with a fingerpost on your left, proceed ahead with wire fence on you right. Pass through a gate to follow a broad track. Go through a gateway and walk round two sides of the field. You cross a small plank bridge. The path ahead may be overgrown before you go over a stile next to a stone-cladded pumping station. The well-waymarked route now goes through the woods. You descend with a fence on your right to turn left at a T-junction and then right at a further junction. You cross a vehicular track before descending to leave the woods over a stile. The path continues between paddock fences to arrive at a major road (A68) which you need to cross with extreme care.

Follow the finger post 'Broomhaugh ½' to go down some steps into a field. Bear right and follow the faint path which leads past trees on the right behind which is Wentworth Care Home. Go over the stile and follow the narrow path which descends quite steeply to meet a minor road (Whiteside Bank). Walk down to the bottom of the road to a junction with the main road (A695). Cross over with care and turn left to The Wellington Hotel, restaurant and bar. The roadside route (**Option B**) coincides here.

Option B (roadside path shorter by 1 mile)

Follow the surfaced path on right-hand side of the A695. When the path ends, cross over to a lay-by to follow the roadside path on the left. After about a further ¾ mile, you reach a major junction at a roundabout. Proceed straight ahead with care to Riding Mill. When convenient, cross over to the right-hand side pavement to reach The Wellington Hotel, restaurant and bar.

A & B

Now continue along the pavement from The Wellington. After about ½ mile, cross over to turn left up the road to Slaley and Shepherds Dene. At its summit you pass some pleasant properties at Beauclerc. After the road bears left, look out on the right for a fingerpost, 'Riding Hills ½' which may be hidden by foliage. Follow the sign and walk up the path with the field boundary hedge on your right. Continue ahead until you arrive at a fence beyond which are the properties at Riding Hills. Turn left and walk a short way to the road. Turn left and follow the road for about 200yds until you reach a junction. Turn right and follow the road as it ascends for about ¾ mile. At the crossroads turn right and proceed passing Prospect Hall Farm, High Level Cottage and High Ash. You arrive at the junction with an access road to Burn Brae Lodge on your right.

Turn left to continue down the road to a junction where you turn left. Walk a short way and turn right at Mount Pleasant Cottage. Follow the steep path through several gates to a minor road (Ladycutter Lane). Cross straight over and go over the stile in the gap of the hedge. Continue with the field edge on your left until you reach a waymarked gate. Go through the gate and follow the path as it descends between the trees to exit onto the main road near Corbridge Station. Follow the roadside path, crossing over to the right-hand side when convenient, eventually to reach the traffic lights at the bridge at Corbridge. Cross over the road and make your way into the car park and the end of this stage of the Trail.

Corbridge

STAGE 4
Corbridge to Warden
7½ miles (12.1km)

Entry/exit points	Corbridge; Dilston 1 mile (1.6km); Hexham ¾ miles (7.7km); Bridge End, Warden 7 ½ miles (12.1km)
Map	See Sketch Map on Page 90 OS Explorer OL43 Hadrian's Wall
Refreshments	Cafés and pubs at Corbridge and Hexham; The Boatside Inn at Warden

From the car park at south end of Corbridge Bridge, go through a gate onto the embankment. Turn left and follow the surfaced path. After about a mile you come to the confluence of the River Tyne and Devil's Water. The surfaced path bears left and continues inland alongside the tributary. After about ¼ mile the surfaced path ends and you join a narrower well-trodden path. You soon arrive at steps and a gate to cross the railway – take extreme care here, cross over and head down some steps. Follow the path until further steps take you to the main road (A695). Turn right and walk along the pavement crossing Dilston Bridge.

Leaving Corbridge

From here you could follow the shorter roadside path alongside the A695 to Hexham. However, for a more interesting and scenic route, shortly after crossing the bridge, as the pavement bears right and you have good visibility of the traffic in both directions, you need to turn left and cross the busy A695 with care. Bear left along the access road that leads to Dilston Physic Garden. Bear right at a B&B and follow the path as it ascends past the Physic Garden on your right and then the Dilston Scout Camp on your left. Go through a gate and continue ahead across a road onto an undulating path that goes uphill through the woods. This path eventually leads to an access road passing Duke's House. About ¼ mile beyond the house, turn right on to a path signposted, 'Hexham ½'.

You pass through a clearing and the path descends quite steeply. Avoid paths off until, eventually, you arrive at an access road. Turn left and follow the undulating road past a pleasant row of cottages with views of the town to your right. The access road then comes out at a road at Fellside where you turn right. Follow the road down the right-hand side as it descends to the junction with the main road (A695). Turn left and then almost immediately cross the road at the pedestrian lights. Turn right and walk a few yards to the pedestrianised Fore Street where you turn left. Follow this street into the Market Place with Hexham Abbey over to your left and the Moot Hall on your right.

Duke's House

Hexham Abbey and market

Bear right to descend the steep Hallstile Bank until it arrives at a set of pedestrian lights. Turn left at the lights and then right to follow the road, crossing over the railway as you make your way towards Tyne Green Country Park. Bear left onto the access road into the riverside park area and then turn right to pass the boathouse to reach the riverside. Now follow the path closest to the river with Tynedale Golf Course on your left. The path continues out of the park onto a surfaced track alongside the Newcastle to Carlisle railway line as well as following the N72 cycle route. After about ½ mile you have a choice of routes:

Option A (if you are not happy with narrow and uneven paths)
Continue straight ahead along the cycle path to the junction with the main road at (**A&B**) below.

Option B (riverside walk subject to erosion)
Turn right at the waymarked fingerpost, go down the steps and follow the path which leads under the A69. Stick to the path closest to the river for about ¾ mile until you are able to take a path down to the river and view the confluence of the North and South Tynes. Now make your way onto the higher path which will take you past a Daft as a Brush marker stone. Continue ahead on the riverside path which needs careful navigation as it becomes quite narrow and uneven in parts. You pass under a railway bridge before the path leads to a property (Ferryman's Cottage) where you need to turn left to arrive at an access road. Turn right and walk to the junction with the main road.

A&B
At the main road, turn right and walk across the bridge to The Boatside Inn at Warden and the end of this stage of Trail. From here, on the left, the Trail continues up the South Tyne (Stages 9-12) and on the right it proceeds up the North Tyne (Stages 5-8).

Choice of routes

STAGE 5
Warden to Barrasford
7 miles (11.3km)

Entry/exit points	Bridge End, Warden; Chollerford 4 miles (6.4km); Barrasford 7 miles (11.3km)
Map	See Sketch Map on Page 42 OS Explorer OL43 Hadrian's Wall
Refreshments	Boatside Inn at Warden; tea room and hotel at Chollerford; Village shop and hotel in Barrasford

Turn right at The Boatside Inn to follow the road known as Homer's Lane, in the direction of Chollerford. After some 2¼ miles, when you reach the junction with the B6319 at Walwick Farm, turn right.

Follow this road for just over a further mile to the junction with the B6318. This is a much busier road, known locally as the Military Road. Cross over with great care and turn right to proceed along the pavement. This stretch of the road is part of the Hadrian's Wall Path.

Chollerford Bridge

You arrive at a roundabout, beyond which stands the George Hotel. Turn right to cross over the road and make your way to Chollerford Bridge. With care, take advantage of the traffic lights to follow the pavement on the left-hand side. At the end of the bridge, turn left, go through the gate and down the stone steps. Now follow the riverside path for about ¾ mile until you reach some steps which take you up to the busy main road (A6079). You now need to follow this road for about two-thirds of a mile, taking great care to use the grass verges as best as possible.

When the road forks at the Church of St Giles at Chollerton, you need to bear left onto a quieter road, direction: 'Wark, Barrasford'. After about ½ mile, leave the road at a waymarked sign on the left. There are several steep paths ahead which can be awkward and slippery to traverse especially after wet weather. Follow the steep tree-lined path down to meet a narrow path. Bear right and after some 20yds turn left to climb through an old gateway. Now descend the steep path with a stream to your left. Go through a kissing gate and into an open area. Turn right and follow tree-line for about 200yds. Bear right to climb again between the trees. You cross a stile as you continue to climb until you reach a junction of paths. Turn left to proceed down a further steep section which may be slippery. Cross the stile at the bottom and walk alongside what is a

North Tyne near Barrasford

Welcome sight

Northumbria Water pumping station. Bear right up the broad access road and after some 200yds turn left onto a faint green path to pass a large tree on your right. The path becomes clearer as it leads to a stile which takes you onto a road. Turn left and, with judicious use of the grass verges, walk up the road just past the Barrasford Arms to the bus shelter and the end of this stage of the Trail.

STAGE 6
Barrasford to Bellingham
13¼ miles (21.3km)

Entry/exit points	Barrasford: Wark 5 miles (8km); Bellingham 13¼ miles (21.3km)
Map	See Sketch Map on Page 30 OS Explorer OL43 Hadrian's Wall OS Explorer OL42 Kielder Water & Forest
Refreshments	Village shop and hotel in Barrasford; pubs and hotel in Wark; cafés and pubs in Bellingham

This stage starts at the bus shelter, a short distance north of the Barrasford Arms. Cross over the road and turn right and follow the pavement to continue out of the centre of Barrasford. Cross back to the other side just beyond the garage to pick up the narrow path alongside the hedge. After about ¾ mile, as the path ends near a pleasant property, you need to continue ahead on the road for about 1¼ miles taking due care.

When you reach Dene View (Burnmouth Cottages, turn left to leave the road and go through a gateway. Follow the wide farm track that descends to rows of young trees. Bear right towards the large field then bear left to proceed on a faint path through the right-hand row of trees. At the end of the plantation, bear right to join a narrow path. You should now be walking with the river now visible on your left. You soon reach a wider track used by vehicles to transport fishermen on the Chipchase Estate (now privately owned and offering facilities for fishing and other events).

Eventually the track becomes an access road and passes properties at Chipchase Mill as it climbs away from the river. There are views of Chipchase Castle before you reach the junction with the main road. Turn left and after about 400yds you pass the entrance to the Castle. You now need to follow the road, again with due care, for about 1½ miles until you reach the bridge over the river to Wark.

Don't cross the bridge, unless you seek refreshments or accommodation, but continue ahead, ignoring roads and paths off, for about ½ mile. You go through a gate with a fingerpost, 'Public Bridleway Low Carry House 1½ miles'. Just after a modern property, you arrive at a waymarked metal gate leading into a field. Go through this gate and continue ahead along the field edge through further gates and fields. (Alternatively you could go through the bridleway gate on your left and follow the very narrow and at times muddy riverside path.)

Fisherman's Bench

As the field edge curves to the right, go through the waymarked gate on your left, bear right and follow the tree-lined path alongside the river. The path becomes a vehicular (fishermen's) track. Just before a fishermen's hut, turn right through a gate and follow the faint path close to the hedge which leads past the farm buildings at Low Carry House to join a farm track. The track becomes a surfaced access road and climbs quite steeply until eventually it joins a local road coming from the right. Continue straight ahead at the junction for about ¼ mile until you cross a stile next to the gate across the road. Now turn left and leave the road through a gate at the fingerpost, 'Redesmouth 2½'.

You need to make your way straight ahead towards the ruined former bastle house and barn on the horizon. You pass a telegraph post to the right of a small rocky outcrop. Keep to the right of the barn and use the ladder stile to join a raised embankment. Turn right and follow wall/fence until you reach a gate at the corner. From here you need to navigate your way carefully across rough ground. Climb diagonally left and then descend passing a clump of trees on your right and make for a waymarked gate in the fence in front of a wooded area.

Once through the double gate, you arrive at the former

Checking the route

Paddle boarding

railway track. Turn right and follow the track for about ½ mile then at a junction of paths turn right and then almost immediately turn left onto a road that leads under the old railway bridge. Follow the access road across the ford. Bear right and climb past a pleasant property on your right, to a gate into Countesspark Wood. For about ¼ mile the path undulates, high above the river, before descending over a small section of duck-boarding. The path leads onto a broader vehicular track close to the river until you reach a narrow path which climbs steeply to a ladder stile.

Once over the stile, turn left to follow the old railway line. You pass former Redesmouth station buildings, now residential properties. This area can be rutted and muddy.

At the end of the former platform you need to turn right and make your way diagonally right to find a path which follows the line of a fence on your right. When you reach the end of the fence at a corner, go through the kissing gate. Continue ahead and follow the access road to the junction with the main road. Turn left and, with extreme care, walk along the busy and twisting road with little verge and very sharp bends under a former railway bridge.

After about ¾ mile, look out for a well-waymarked gateway on the left. Go through the gate and follow the farm track towards the river. The track bears right as you continue with river close-by. Gates take you across two fields. What becomes an access road leads you past some holiday cottages at Boat Farm. As the road bears right next to two cottages, you need to turn left to leave the road and go through a kissing gate. The path soon descends to the riverside and eventually the path makes its way, on an officially diverted path, around a large property. At the junction with a road, turn left and continue a short distance to the Riverside Garage where you bear right to walk a short way uphill to the Boer War Memorial, the Rose and Crown pub, the Rocky Road Café and the end of this stage of the Trail in Bellingham.

In Bellingham

STAGE 7
Bellingham to Kielder Dam
12¼ miles (19.7km)

Entry/exit points	Bellingham); Lanehead 4¼ miles (6.8km); Falstone 10¼ miles (16.5km); Kielder Dam (Yarrowmoor car park) 12 ¼ miles (19.7km)
Map	See Sketch Map on Page 20 OS Explorer OL42 Kielder Water & Forest
Refreshments	Range of hotels, pubs and cafés in Bellingham; tearoom and hotel in Falstone

From the war memorial, close to the Rose and Crown pub, walk down hill to the Riverside Garage. Turn right in the direction, 'Riverside Walk (North) 2'. Now follow the path with the river on your left for about a mile. After leaving a wooded area, you continue close to the river until you exit onto a main road. Take great care as you walk up this often busy road for about a mile before turning first left down a minor road opposite a large walled property (Charlton House).

Proceed along this very minor road which leads through a cluster of properties, and farm buildings (Newton). Turn right under a bridge and then immediately left. Follow along two sides of the field boundary. Continue on the access road passing a few properties to a T-junction. Turn right, being aware again of the traffic at Lanehead. and walk up 150yds before turning left, 'Donkleywood 3'. Follow this quieter road as it descends for about a mile. At a sharp right-angle bend and a small grassy area, a fingerpost on the left next to a ladder stile, indicates, 'The Hott ½'. Here you have a choice of routes:

Option A (this continues along the narrow quiet road)
Continue along the gated road and, after passing the level crossing at the former Thorneyburn Station, as the road

turns right, you reach the point where Option B emerges (Hadyad Ford).

Option B (for the more adventurous, initially rough and boggy)
Cross the ladder stile and make your way down the field as best as you can to the tunnel in the embankment ahead. After going through the short tunnel under the dismantled railway, bear right and follow the edge of the open green space for about 75yds before picking up a faint path that descends to the North Tyne. Turn right to follow the river upstream. You pass the Hott Bridge before proceeding along the riverside to rejoin the road (Hadyad Ford).

Under the old railway

A&B
Continue along the road for about a mile and shortly after passing some farm buildings you need to cross a stile on your left that leads into a wooded area. Take care as you

River reappears

contour down to a small footbridge and climb steeply out from the aptly named, 'Rough Cleugh'. Go over the stile, turn left and follow the field boundary to a fenced area where you need to go through a set of gates. Descend steeply to follow a fence on your right. Go over a small burn before climbing with the fence still on your right. Go over the stile and bear left to follow the direction of the waymark up the field. Head for the tallest tree then make your way to cross a stile to the right of a wide gate. Then continue ahead past the property on your right (Camp Cottage) to cross a stile before going through a wooden gate. The path continues with fencing on your right as you descend towards the river.

Follow the path with the river on your left to find a stile next to a gate at the corner of a field. Once over the stile proceed diagonally right across the field to pass a prominent tree. Bear right to a pair of stone gates where you join a farm track and turn right as it leads over a former railway bridge before reaching some cottages. Proceed between the buildings and cross the stone stile into

Falstone hospitality

Kielder Dam

Donkleywood. Turn left and follow the road out of the village for the next 1¾ miles into Falstone.

At a junction at another former railway bridge, turn left and walk under the bridge. You pass St Peter's Church and walk between the Blackcock Inn and the Tearoom. Leave the road after about 40yds to turn right between stone pillars next to a narrow gateway to pick up a path parallel to the road. This path leads down to the river near the road bridge. Turn right and continue alongside the river passing a stone sculpture. You join a road where you bear left to pass a tennis court and a children's play area. Proceed along the road, ignoring paths off. Eventually as you approach some farm buildings you go through a gate and follow the track which bears left. At a crossing of paths, turn left and continue straight ahead as the track gradually climbs, before a surfaced road leads past a plaque and stone monument commemorating the opening of the Kielder Dam. Turn left to cross the dam wall at the far end of which you arrive at the Yarrowmoor Car Park and the end of this stage of the Trail.

STAGE 8
Kielder Dam to the Source of the North Tyne
15½ miles (20km)

Entry/exit points	Kielder Dam (Yarrowmoor car park; Tower Knowe ¾ mile (1.3km); Leaplish 5½ miles (9km); Matthew's Linn 7¾ miles (12.5km); Kielder 12 miles (19.4km); Roadside on C200 (GR604974) at the England-Scotland Border some 250yds beyond Deadwater Farm 15½ miles (25km)
Map	See Sketch Map on Page 10 OS Explorer OL42 Kielder Water & Forest
Refreshments	Visitor centres at Leaplish and Tower Knowe; The Anglers Arms pub and Kielder Castle Visitor Centre at Kielder Village

From the Yarrowmoor Car Park on the south side of the dam follow the surfaced Lakeside Way path signed, 'Kielder

Kielder Water

Castle 14½ miles (23km); Tower Knowe Centre ¾ miles (1.2km); Kielder Waterside) 8½ miles (13.7km)'.

After passing the Tower Knowe Centre the Trail winds around the lakeside passing close to Kielder Yacht Club, descending steeply to cross a small bridge over the Clanecleugh Burn. The path then zig-zags up through the trees onto forest paths on Bulls Crag. It is possible perhaps more so, for cyclists, to continue round the Crag and enjoy some fine views. However, the DAAB waymarks follow a shorter route across the Crag to 'Freya's Cabin'. From here you descend to pass the Water Ski Club before reaching Kielder Waterside with all its amenities.

Freya's Cabin

There is a small minor road section near the access to Hawkhirst Scout Activity Centre. You then pass Matthew's Linn with the Calvert Trust Activity Centre.

Through Kielder Forest

The Trail then does a loop around the long inlet of the Lewis Burn which includes passing under the C200 road bridge and crossing a neatly curved bridge before returning back through Kielder Forest towards the lakeside. Continue following the signs ignoring paths off unless you wish to visit the splendid Kielder Viaduct.

The path descends to go through a circular parking area before you turn left. You cross a road in the direction, 'Kielder Castle & Village ½', with Butteryhaugh Bridge to your right. Follow the path which leads to a road where you turn left and walk a short way, before crossing over the road with care and taking the minor road that leads to the visitor centre at Kielder Castle. However, unless you wish to visit these facilities, turn left to pass the Anglers Arms. Continue ahead through the campsite to a junction with the main road. Turn right and proceed with care for about 250yds before turning left onto a broad track just before the former chapel building. After about a further 275yds bear right onto what was formerly part of the Border Counties Railway and is now a 'Shared Trail'.

The Shared Trail goes through a gate at Bells Burn cottage and continues for about a mile to pass the former Deadwater Station, now a private residence.

Go through a gate and continue along the Shared Trail for about ¼ mile to the treeline where you turn right through a gate. Follow the permissive path and go through a further gate. Cross the C200 road with great care as it is much used by timber haulage vehicles. Go through the gate and climb up the path to reach the stone sculpture which marks the source of the North Tyne and the end of this stage of the Trail.

Brian Burnie and team

STAGE 9
Warden to Haydon Bridge
6½ miles (10.5km)

Entry/exit points	Bridge End, Warden; Haydon Bridge ½ miles (10.5km)
Map	See Sketch Map on Page 84 OS Explorer OL43 Hadrian's Wall
Refreshments	The Boatside Inn at Warden; Pubs/hotels in Haydon Bridge

From the front of the Boatside Inn, proceed up the road (B6319) towards Fourstones. After about ¾ mile you pass the Fourstones Paper complex. Go through the gate on the left just before the level crossing lights. The river becomes visible again, as you follow the narrow and

Paul and Peter Leaving The Boatside Inn

uneven path. At times the path bears away from the river where there is private land reserved for fishing. As you return closer to the river you join a broader path. You pass a large house and an access road on the right. Continue straight ahead on the narrow path with a fence on your right. At some farm buildings and a cottage you arrive at a junction of paths. Continue straight ahead on the clear green path or follow the parallel narrower riverside path.

After about ¼ mile, as the path narrows and comes to an end, you need to turn left through a gap in a wall. Proceed along the riverside for a short distance and then clamber down over a stony section where the Newbrough Burn enters the South Tyne. Bear right under the railway bridge and turn right to go up some steps.

Turn almost immediately left, follow a track through the woods and through a gap in the fence onto an access road.

Turn left and proceed a short way to return to the B6319 at a parking space.

Turn left and follow road for about 3 miles. The road is generally quiet but due care needs to be taken. As you approach Haydon Bridge, with the railway embankment evident on your left and some industrial units on the right, look out for a tunnel under the embankment. Go through the tunnel and turn immediately right. Proceed along the path for a couple of hundred yards until you join a surfaced path and pass a picnic area. You soon reach a junction with a main road where you turn right and then almost immediate right again into Church Street. Continue ahead, passing the War Memorial and St Cuthbert's Churh, to reach Haydon Bridge Station and the end of this stage of the Trail.

Following the road

Haydon Bridge Church and War Memorial

STAGE 10
Haydon Bridge to Haltwhistle
12 miles (19.3km)

Entry/exit points	**Haydon Bridge; National Trust car park at Allen Banks 4 miles (6.4km); Beltingham 5 miles (8km); Bardon Mill 6 miles (9.6km); Haltwhistle 12 miles (19.3km)**
Map	**See Sketch Map on Page 72** **OS Explorer OL43 Hadrian's Wall**
Refreshments	**A selection of possibilities at Haydon Bridge, Bardon Mill and Haltwhistle**

From Haydon Bridge Station turn left and go down Church Street. At the end of the street you need to cross over the road and go over the pedestrianised bridge. Turn right to proceed along John Martin Street/Shaftoe Street. After about 150yds turn right to leave the main road and walk down Lands End Road. Continue ahead on the minor road passing housing and an information panel about the artist John Martin. The road leads under the A69 Haydon Bridge bypass and continues with fields on either side. Leave the road at a fingerpost, 'Allen Banks 1½', and follow an access road into Lees Farm. Turn left to pass some cottages. Go through a gate at the fingerpost 'Allen Banks 1' and turn right.

Follow a green path for a few yards before bearing left to climb up the steep hillside and make your way past a clump of trees on your right. Then go diagonally right to cross the stone wall over a waymarked ladderstile. Continue up the hillside to the left-hand side of the woods (Lees Heugh Wood). At the top of the rise, go through the gate and continue ahead towards a ladderstile in a broken wall. Once over the stile, follow the green track down to a gate/stile onto an access road to Tedcastle Farm that lies down to the right.

However, you need to turn left and walk up to join a minor road. Turn right and follow the road as it descends for about 400yds. Shortly after it bears right look out for a gate on the left (a National Trust sign is half-hidden in the bushes). Here you have a choice of routes which may depend on weather conditions and time available:

Option A (generally quiet road walk)
Continue down the road for about a mile, steeply for the first ¾ mile, to arrive at the entrance to the National Trust Allen Banks and Staward Gorge car park and toilets, located within the former walled garden of Ridley Hall where both options converge. See A&B below.

Option B (scenic woodland walk)
Leave the road and go through the gate and walk ahead on the green path. Go through a kissing gate into the National Trust estate and a series of permissive paths (generally indicated by purple waymarks). You need to turn immediately right.

You are going to walk through the woods for about a mile. The descent is fairly gradual for about the first 500yds. At a junction of paths, you need to bear right as indicated by the RTT waymark. The path goes down more steeply for about 75yds to a purple waymark where you need to turn right. Continue downhill until you reach a gate. Go through the gate, bear right and follow the field edge until you reach a gate where you turn right. Now continue ahead along the field edge for about 125yds and bear left to leave the field and walk under a road bridge. Go through the gate, turn immediately right and walk across the bridge. After about 150yds you arrive at the entrance to the National Trust Allen Banks & Staward Gorge car park and toilets where both options converge.

A&B
Continue along the road for a further ¼ mile to reach a road junction at the entrance to Ridley Hall (owned by the Bowes-Lyon family until 2017, then a boarding school, now a private residence). Bear left in the direction 'Beltingham' and continue ahead as the road climbs. After a further ¼ mile or so walkers leave the road at a fingerpost on the right, 'Beltingham ¼' and go through a gate into a field. Proceed ahead along the top of the field keeping close to the fence on your left. The path bears left as it descends steeply between the trees, crosses a burn and then climbs to meet a road at the hamlet of Beltingham. Turn right and follow the road past St Cuthbert's Church. Take care as the

Beltingham Church

road bears sharp left and descends steeply. The road levels out and after about ¼ mile you arrive at a gate on the right leading into a wooded area. Here walkers have the choice of routes:

Option A (visit the pleasant Wildlife's Trust's Northumberland Nature Reserve and walk along the riverside, however, this may be impassable following heavy rain and flooding)

Go through the gate, pass the information panel 'Calaminarian Grassland' and bear left to pick up a path to the riverside. Care needs to be taken with tree roots and overhanging branches. Ignore paths off and keep close to the river. After about ½ mile you rejoin the minor road at a clearing close to a footbridge.

Link with Bardon Mill

Option B (easier if time is short)
Continue straight ahead down the road to a clearing close to a footbridge where A & B converge.

A & B

Don't cross the footbridge unless you wish to visit Bardon Mill but instead continue along the road for about a mile. Shortly after it climbs past Bridge Cottage, leave the road and turn right to pass some farm buildings and the fortified manor house of Willimoteswick. Continue down the steep vehicular track. The track levels out and you pass a cottage and some outbuildings. Go over a stile, proceed along the track for about 200yds and as the road bears right, leave the track and turn left to continue up a grassy bank to a gate that leads into Haughstrother Wood.

Follow the forest track, ignoring paths off. The track, which may be rutted and muddy, descends and you leave the forest via a gate. Continue ahead along the track until eventually you cross a stone bridge. Turn right to pass some barns and outbuildings at Shankfoot. You join the minor Unthank Road which leads past East Unthank Farm and then Unthank Hall. After a further ¾ mile you reach a junction where you turn right. Continue past the dwellings of Plenmeller. As the road descends, ignore a path off to the left (South Tyne Trail), and go through a second gate on the left just before reaching the main road (A69). Proceed along the surfaced Cycleway 68.

You come to a junction of paths with the ruins of Bellister Castle on your left. Cross over the road to go through a gateway next to a cattle grid. Bear left onto an old road (Bellister Road). You pass a fingerpost on your left, 'Bellister Bank ½'. (You will need to return to this point to continue on Stage 11 Haltwhistle to Alston.) However, to walk from here into Haltwhistle, continue along the old road as it bears right under the A69 road bridge. From here you have a choice of routes:

Option A (riverside path liable to flooding after rain)
After about 40yds beyond the road bridge, turn left at a fingerpost, 'Bellister Haugh ½'. Go through the gap in the fence and follow the path down to the riverside. Follow the path downstream, climbing after about 100yds to cross over an access road and then back down to the riverside. Continue on the riverside path for a further 700yds or so before leaving the riverside to climb to the end of a bridge. Turn left, walk across the bridge and go under the Boat Lane railway bridge to arrive at a road junction where both options converge. See A&B below.

Nearing the A69 at Haltwhistle

Option B (along quiet old road, Bellister Road)
After going under A69 road bridge, continue ahead on the old road for about half a mile. Ignore paths off until you pass a property where you turn left and cross a bridge over the South Tyne and go under the Boat Lane railway bridge to arrive at a road junction.

A&B
Followers of either option turn left at the road junction. Proceed a short distance, and at a crossroads, turn left into Haltwhistle Station car park. This is the end of this stage of the Trail and the town centre and amenities lie very close at hand.

STAGE 11
Haltwhistle to Alston
13¾ miles (22.1km)

Entry/exit points	Haltwhistle; Coanwood Station car park 4 ¼ miles (6.8km); Slaggyford 9¼ miles (14.9km); Alston 13¾ miles (22.1km)
Map	See Sketch Map on Page 60 OS Explorer OL43 Hadrian's Wall OS Explorer OL31 North Pennines
Refreshments	Several cafés and hotels/ pubs in Haltwhistle and Alston

From Haltwhistle railway station, walk to the crossroads, with The Railway Inn just beyond, and turn right. (From Platform 2 you can access the Trail directly by following the sign, 'Way out avoiding footbridge'.) Proceed a short way before turning right to go under the railway line at Boat Lane. A bridge then takes you over the South Tyne and a choice of routes:

Option A (riverside path liable to flooding after very heavy rain)
Turn immediately right at the end of the bridge and make your way down the stony path to the riverside. Follow the river upstream. You need to cross over an access road before continuing along the riverside. After about ½ mile, just before the A69 road bridge, you need to turn left up a stony path. Go through a gap in the fence and join an old road (Bellister Road). Turn right and walk a few yards to the bridge under the A69 where you continue at A&B below.

Option B (very quiet access road)
After crossing the bridge over the South Tyne, continue ahead to a junction. Turn right and proceed along the old road (Bellister Road), for about a half a mile, ignoring paths off, to the bridge under the A69. Continue as below.

Haltwhistle riverside

A & B

Almost immediately after passing under the A69 bridge, leave the road and turn right at a waymarked fingerpost ('Bellister Bank ½'). Proceed down the stepped-path and turn left at the riverside. Follow the path which climbs gently parallel to the minor road. After about ¼ mile go up a series of steep steps and turn right. You pass through two gates and the path becomes fenced on both sides. You are now on the National Trust Bellister Estate permissive path.

Follow the path, through the trees, ignoring paths off until you exit onto the minor road. Now follow the road for about a mile. When you see the pedestrian bridge go through a gate, don't cross the bridge, but bear left and follow the path with the fence on your left. Featherstone Castle appears on the left. The path leads past a stone pillar, the remains of a prisoner of war camp. Follow the surfaced track alongside the river being aware of danger from erosion. The track exits through a gate onto a road. Turn right, walk a few yards, cross the road with care, and turn left through a gateway. Continue ahead down the vehicular track passing some trees as the track levels off. The path becomes faint and you need to aim to pass close to a clump of trees on your right. Make your way towards a junction of paths at an isolated property. You now have a choice of routes:

Across the field

Option A (To cross the South Tyne via the Lambley Viaduct, if you have a head for heights).
At the isolated property, turn left and climb up the broad track that leads through a gate to a junction. Turn right into a small parking area and proceed straight ahead for just over ¼ mile to the Lambley Viaduct. Walk across the viaduct which unfortunately is blocked at the end. You then need to turn right and descend a series of steps to a junction of paths at a fingerpost. Turn right in the direction 'South Tyne Trail (North)' to reach the riverside where you turn right and follow the path under the viaduct until you climb back to reach the former railway line. See A&B below.

Option B (Slightly shorter but less spectacular).
Should you not wish to walk across the viaduct, instead of turning left at the isolated cottage, you need to turn right and follow the path across a small plank bridge into a field. Turn immediately right to leave the track and enter a field. Walk down the field towards the riverside, keeping midway between a telegraph pole and the right-hand field edge, to a waymarked post on a ridge. Turn left and continue ahead. You pass through a metal gate/stile before reaching a footbridge. After crossing the footbridge, follow the path which leads up some steep steps to a fingerpost at a junction of paths. Turn left and follow the sign, 'South Tyne Trail (North)'. The path leads under the viaduct to join the former railway line. See A&B below.

A & B

To continue on the Trail you need to follow the former railway line, ignoring paths off, for about 4 miles to a locked gate across the railway line. Turn left and then immediately right to follow the short diversion back to the level crossing gates at Slaggyford Station, the current end of the South Tynedale Railway.

View from the viaduct

To continue on the Trail, go through the gate on the left just before the level crossing. Follow the permissive path parallel to the railway line for about 4¾ miles to arrive at Alston Station and the end of this section of the Trail.

Along the line

STAGE 12
Alston to the Source of the South Tyne
9¾ miles (15.7km)*

Entry/exit points	Alston; Garrigill 4¾ miles (7.7km); Gateway/cattle grid at the end of the minor road from Garrigill 9¾ miles (15.7km)
Map	See Sketch Map on Page 50 OS Explorer OL31 North Pennines
Refreshments	Pubs and cafés in Alston; village shop in Garrigill

(As there is no unauthorised vehicular road access to the marker stones, you need to retrace your steps down the track for 2 miles to a cattle grid beyond which cars can be parked- otherwise you need to walk a further 2 miles to Garrigill!)

Exit from Alston railway station and turn right at the main road (A686). Proceed straight ahead, ignoring the left turn onto the A689, and continue past the Alston House Hotel. After ¼ mile leave the road to turn left towards the Cottage Hospital. Walk up the access road and turn first right towards the Youth Hostel. After about 40yds, bear right at the fingerpost, 'Pennine Way, South Tyne Trail, Garrigill 3¾'. Follow the path with the river below and the youth hostel and the cemetery above on your left. Go through a small wooden gate and continue along the clear path which takes you over several stiles, a footbridge, gaps in walls, further stiles and the occasional property on your left.

Proceed ahead passing a wall and a copse of trees on your left. Eventually, after crossing a stile, the path leads across three fields. Follow the left-hand boundary and after another stile, look out for a stile next to a gate on your left. Turn left here and walk past the farm buildings at Bleagate. Bear right to leave the road at a fingerpost. Follow the path up with the wall on your left. Go over a gated stile and continue along the path as it descends diagonally right to go over a stile and then through a gap in a wall at a small waymarked post. Turn left and follow the wall towards the farmhouse. Bear right to a stone bench. Follow the faint path, just below the bench, as it contours left towards the trees. Go over a small plank bridge and a stile and continue down the narrow and stony path as it descends into a field.

Proceed ahead along the field edge to the end of the field and then bear right to pick up a farm track. Follow the track through the

Garrigill Church

remains of a wall and continue for about 400yds until you reach a footbridge over the South Tyne. Cross the bridge and turn left. Walk ahead and follow the river, crossing a number of stiles. The path climbs away from the riverside and you pass some wasteland before exiting onto a minor road. Turn left and continue along the road for about ½ mile to the village green in Garrigill.

Continue ahead, ignoring the road to the left, past St John's Church and keep left at a junction as the road climbs steeply out of Garrigill. Leave the road through a gate on the left at a fingerpost, just beyond Crossgill Lodge. Go down the track, cross the stone bridge (Windshaw Bridge) and turn right. (From here onwards to the source of the South Tyne there are numerous stiles some of which are quite high!) Follow the riverside to a corner where the South Tyne is met by the Ash Gill. Follow the path alongside the tributary to arrive at a bridge. After crossing the bridge walk straight ahead crossing over a path leading up towards a property.

Continue ahead on the clear path which eventually passes a fence on your right and a young plantation. You cross a small plank bridge and the path may be overgrown as you head towards a wall, which you need to cross via a high stile to the right. This stile is located up the bankside and you may need to scramble to reach it! Continue ahead across the field for about ¼ mile, crossing a stile and an access road before going through a gateway to pass the barns of Hole House Farm on your right. Follow the wire fence on your right after which you need to pick up a farm track on your right which leads you through a gate. Bear right to walk closer to the riverside. After about ½ mile you cross another access road with a property (Tynehead) on your left and you cross a small stream (Chargill).

Continue ahead past the remains of some buildings as the path climbs and becomes faint and rough. Ahead you will see the dramatic Dorthgill Falls. Care needs to be taken as the path narrows and becomes stony and at times muddy. You cross a stile and in a short distance make your way down, past a large farm building on your right, to reach a road/track. Turn left and follow the track for 1¼ mile to reach the stones which mark the source of the South Tyne and the end of the River Tyne Trail.

Congratulations, and don't forget to take some photographs before commencing your way back to the cattle grid when hopefully you have transport to take you back to Garrigill!

Dorthgill Falls

Journey's end

Footnote: For details of the River Tyne Cycle Route created by Eric Stewart, see **www.daftasabrush.org.uk/tyne-trail/**